MISSION

to

LITTLE GRAND RAPIDS

Life with the Anishinabe
1927 to 1938

Father,

You lived it.
You wrote it.
Here is your book.

From your Children

MISSION

to

LITTLE GRAND RAPIDS

Life with the Anishinabe
1927 to 1938

A Memoir by the Reverend Luther L. Schuetze

Creative Connections Publishing

National Library of Canada Cataloguing in Publication Data

Schuetze, Luther L., b. 1891.
Mission to Little Grand Rapids

Includes bibliographical references and index.
ISBN 1-894694-02-3

1. Schuetze, Luther L., b. 1891.
2. Ojibwa Indians--Missions--Manitoba--Little Grand Rapids.
3. Missionaries--Manitoba--Little Grand Rapids--Biography.
4. United Church of Canada--Clergy--Biography. I. Title.
BX9883.S32A3 2001   266'.792'092   C2001-910185-6

Research and Editing: Alvina Block
Editor: Bernard Shalka
Book and Cover Design: Leon Phillips
Indexer: Renée Fossett

First printing: June 2001

Creative Connections Publishing
Suite 212 - 1656 Duranleau Street • Granville Island
• Vancouver, B.C. V6H 3S4 • 604-688-0320 • toll-free 1-877-688-0320 •
email: ccpublishing@axion.net
www.creativeconnectionspublishing.com

Affiliated Publishers in
Vancouver • Calgary • Milwaukee • Denver

Cover photographs:

Background - Little Grand Rapids
Inset - Luther chatting with Deer Lakers
after a church service

Printed by Friesens, Altona, Manitoba, Canada

"May this be a means of helping others to find their faith and have it strengthened..."

Rev. L.L. Schuetze, from his prologue, 1964

The Lutheran Church in Joinville, Brazil, where Luther was christened, c. 1900

Table of Contents

List of Illustrations

All photographs come from the Schuetze family album unless otherwise indicated.

Photographs

Maps

Acknowledgements

To me, it was a magical place where childhood fantasies and dreams were formed. I thank God for putting my father at Little Grand Rapids when I was young. My family and I have returned there several times and have greatly appreciated the warm reception by our friends.

Christina Moar, daughter of former Chief Alex Boucher and a classmate of mine in father's school, was there to greet us when my parents were along. George Quantrill of Little Grand Rapids Lodge was very hospitable, and airport manager Dorothy Quantrill, daughter of William Keeper, was my resource person for the Anishinabe language.

We also received a friendly welcome in Poplar River, where Eleanor Lambert was a gracious host, and Fred Lambert took us out to visit the spot where the Schuetze Trading Post had been.

This book, which is based on the original manuscript written by my father, has come into being through the efforts of my brother Ernest, myself, and a number of other individuals and organizations.

After my daughter Gaye typed the manuscript, Ernest took the disk, scanned the photographs and maps and created the first design of the family edition. Over a period of five years he made many revisions to this document. Shortly after producing his final version he passed away.

Alvina Block, M.A., provided indispensable research and editing, then wrote the introduction, to which I added some comments. I also wrote the foreword, the epilogue, and Appendix A.

Professor Jennifer Brown of the University of Winnipeg gave us much-appreciated support and made numerous valuable suggestions.

Bernard Shalka did the final editing, Leon Phillips saw to the final design and map work, and Denise De Leebeeck, Ernest's daughter, looked after the proofreading. Their meticulous labours were co-ordinated by Jo Blackmore of Creative Connections Publishing.

The Roman Catholic Mission at Berens River, Manitoba, sent us the photo of John Duck. Permission to use this photograph, as well as excerpts from the memoir of Brother Leach, was kindly given by the Oblates of Mary Immaculate in St. Boniface, Manitoba.

The American Philosophical Society in Philadelphia provided a copy of the picture of "Kitegas" from its Hallowell Collection.

The Centre of Rupert's Land Studies at the University of Winnipeg saw the need for an index and made a generous contribution towards its production by Renée Fossett.

Herman L. Schuetze

Foreword

Born to German immigrant parents in Brazil, educated in basic medicine and theology in Germany, acclimatized to the Canadian bush by years of farm work and canoe travel after the family relocated to Manitoba—Luther Schuetze could have been created to take the Gospel to the Anishinabe people of Manitoba. However, by the time he received the call from the fledgling United Church of Canada, Luther was married, had three sons with a fourth on the way, and had built a thriving business as a fur trader.

"Well then, I will pray about it and see what I can do," he recalls himself answering the Church's officials. And so it came about that Luther Schuetze took on the task of establishing a permanent United Church Mission at a place called Little Grand Rapids.

Here is Luther's report of those first years of his ministry under the auspices of the United Church. He writes of this experience as of a golden age, of times long past when he was at his prime. But as he is retired and into his seventies when he puts pen to paper, the events crowd upon themselves, and their order may not always be correct. But this much is certain: they did happen as he has written them.

You will find a sense of pride in what he accomplished, or rather what God has done through him, so there is always that attempt to keep from boasting, and to give the credit to the God who prepared him for this task and saw him through it. One can only marvel at how God works, for He had prepared this man to do this work for Him through the years.

Baptized Lothar Ludwig Schütze in Joinville, Brazil, the young boy played in the jungle fringes around the town and went with his father on trips into the jungle's depths. And so was born in him the love of God's natural world, which he shared with his papa.

When the family moved to a farm in Canada, near Winnipeg, their names were anglicized, and teenaged Lothar became Luther Schuetze. The hired hands taught him about farming, and he came to know and love horses, and learned to drive them. This skill was later put to good use, as Luther became a teamster, hauling frozen whitefish from ice-covered Lake Winnipeg to the nearest railhead. Thus, when you read of his use of horses in mission-building, you will understand how God had prepared him to do this kind of work.

Luther's love of nature, born in the jungles of Brazil, deepened as he and his brother got acquainted with the Manitoba bush. They paddled its waterways, hunted, fished, and trapped, learning to survive through its seasons. They built their own cabins, snowshoes, and paddles. They lived through the winters, trapping fur-bearing animals for pelts. The brothers adapted to the land and loved it. And so again, God was preparing Luther for what lay ahead.

As a young man Luther exulted in his strength, vigor, and freedom in this new world of Canada. He lived life to the fullest—perhaps too much so. One winter he almost died, probably in part because of his excesses. But this low point turned him around so that God could use him for His purpose. Thus was born in him a new spirit, a zeal to do God's will rather than his own. And so, prepared in this way too, Luther waited for the call.

It came in 1926. The United Church of Canada, formed the previous year by the union of three Protestant denominations, was looking for a preacher-teacher who could establish a Mission at a small settlement up the Berens River, near the Ontario border. Now in his prime of life, Luther decided to start a new one. What follows is his recollection of how he answered the call to do God's will in Little Grand Rapids.

One can only marvel at how God works. He had pre-pared this man to do this work for Him through many years. And He wasn't finished with him yet. Let the reader be aware that this book tells the story of Luther's first eleven years of service only. But in these years you may see, as you read, how God honed him for the future.

The United Church has come far since the time it sent out missionaries to bring the Gospel of Christ to First Nations peoples. Today Little Grand Rapids is being served by a layman from the community who may take courses that lead to ordination in the United Church, just as his father before him had done.

However, unlike in earlier times, ordination training for First Nations candidates for ministry recognizes that cultural and spiritual backgrounds must be taken into account. In Manitoba this training takes place at a special facility called the Dr. Jessie Saulteaux Resource Centre. Furthermore, the First Nations clergy and delegates now have an All Native Circle Conference, where they deal with their concerns in their own way.

Readers who wish to know more about how the United Church of Canada has changed with respect to the rights and traditions of First Nations peoples are referred to the Epilogue.

A final comment is appropriate respecting the word "pagan," as it appears following. In the old days the term was commonly used to identify non-Christian people. Today we recognize that First Nations spirituality is to be respected, and we walk beside those with faith traditions different from our own.

Herman L. Schuetze, November 2000

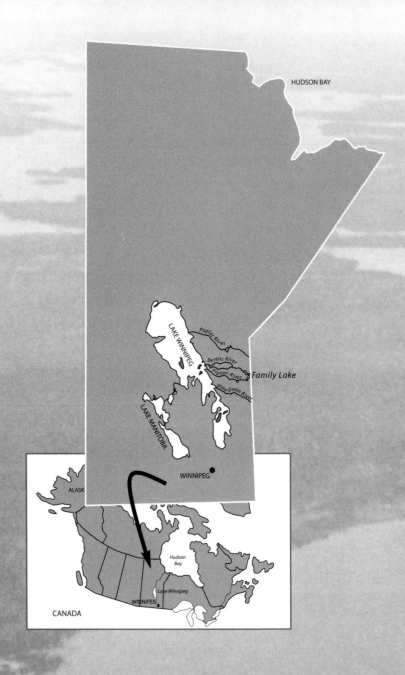

INTRODUCTION: AN OVERVIEW

The Place

Little Grand Rapids Reserve is located 268 air kilometres (167 mi.) northeast of Winnipeg on the shores of Family Lake, near the Manitoba/Ontario border. The community is spread out over eight kilometres (five mi.) along the north end of the east shore of the lake (see map, p. 43). On February 25, 1930, an Order-in-Council granted Little Grand Rapids separate band status. The people refer to Little Grand Rapids as Mishay Powitik, which means Grand Rapids.

In 1801, David Sanderson came to Little Grand Rapids from the Albany Fort and established a winter trading post for the Hudson's Bay Company, calling the area "Big Fall."[1] In 1816, Donald Sutherland arrived from Fort York to establish a palisade fort, and he renamed Big Fall as "Great Falls." When William McKay, the post manager at Berens River, established an outpost in 1848, he changed Great Falls to "Grand Rapids." In subsequent years, Grand Rapids became known as "Grand Rapids of the Berens River," to distinguish it from the place called Grand Rapids on Lake Winnipeg at the mouth of the Saskatchewan River. This led to the names "Little Grand Rapids" and "Big Grand Rapids." The former name remains intact, while the latter has been simplified to "Grand Rapids."

The People

The members of the band at Little Grand Rapids originated around Lake Superior, and were possibly driven north by a more warlike southern tribe. They describe themselves as Anishinabe, which simply means "the people." The original language of the band is Ojibwa, modified over time by contact with English and French. "Bonjour, bonjour," is a popular greeting. The term Saulteaux, used to describe the Anishinabe in Luther Schuetze's memoir, originated at Sault St. Marie where they were active in canoe work for traders heading west.

Aerial photograph of Little Grand Rapids

On September 20, 1875, the Berens River area, which included Little Grand Rapids, Pikangikum, Poplar River, and Bloodvein, came under Treaty 5. In 1876, Jacob Berens, the chief of Berens River, and Na-Na-quawa-na-qua, the principal Indian residing at Little Grand Rapids, requested that a reserve be created for Little Grand Rapids. At the time there were 170 band members, including 62 of the Lac Seul Band which originated from the Savanne agency close to Sioux Lookout, Ontario. The band members asked for cattle, implements, and four square miles of hay land on the Pigeon River. The request for the reserve was granted, but Alexander Morris, the lieutenant governor of Manitoba, didn't think the band was ready to have cattle. He wrote: "The region in which they live is a very bad, uninviting one, with swamps, rocks and only patches of good soil."[2]

The reserve was surveyed in September of 1888 by A.W. Ponton. At that time the band was living in tents, except for headman Dick Green, who had a house. Band members had small gardens, and Dick Green also had a quarter acre of potatoes and a stable for wintering cattle.[3] However, in 1903 Indian Agent S.J. Jacks reported that the band had no cattle. They had requested a two-year-old heifer and a yearling bull in order to make a fresh start. Jacks wrote that there were 137 band members who lived mostly in tents. He described the children thus: "I never saw a finer or a healthier lot of children than in this band."[4]

The band depended upon trapping and fishing for its livelihood. Also, most of the men worked for the Hudson's Bay Company either directly or indirectly. A brief history of the Hudson's Bay Company in Manitoba is contained in Appendix A.

Methodist Church Presence

Jacob Berens (c.1829–1917), of Berens River, became a Christian and was baptized in 1861 by George McDougall, the Methodist missionary at Norway House. Through Berens's efforts, Egerton R. Young came to Berens

River as a resident missionary in 1873.[5] Methodist missionaries believed that the Ojibwa [Anishinabe] were "extremely obdurate to conversion" in comparison with the Cree.[6] However, by 1892 all the residents of Berens River were Christians, according to official reports.

In 1899 the Methodist Conference asked missionary James A. McLachlan, who had been at Berens River since 1890, to minister to Little Grand Rapids as part of his mandate.[7]

In 1905, Little Grand Rapids and Pikangikum were listed with the stations of the Manitoba Conference of the Methodist Church. In the 1905 sessional papers, Indian Agent Neil Gilmour described the Anishinabe of Little Grand Rapids as pagan, but noted that the Methodist Church was establishing a mission and arranging to conduct a school for the education of the children. The Methodist Church had sent William Ivens (later involved in the Social Gospel movement) to Little Grand as minister/teacher in 1904. Joseph F. Woodsworth followed him in 1908.

In 1909, while Joseph Jones ministered at the reserve, church membership fell from fifty-four to zero. Perhaps Jones was the missionary who, according to Luther Schuetze, "took forcible action" against drum dances. The Rev. Roy Taylor followed in 1910, J.H. Wilding in 1911, and Alfred G. Johnson in 1914.[8] It would appear that the Church was seeking a missionary for Little Grand Rapids between 1917 and 1926. However, records indicate nine baptisms and one marriage in 1919.

From 1920 to 1927, the records show that Little Grand Rapids had ten Methodist families with twelve members (presumably meaning members of the Methodist Church). J.J. Everett was the teacher/missionary in 1927, and Luther Schuetze served as a supplier.

As detailed in Chapter Four, Schuetze took over as missionary and teacher in 1928. His annual salary was $800. The next year he was called a missionary/preacher, and his salary increased to $1,400. The minutes of the Methodist Church for 1929 show the same number of

Methodist families and church members as in 1927. There was one marriage.

Education

From 1904 to 1907, William Ivens was the missionary teacher at Little Grand Rapids, under the supervision of Berens River. Ivens began a day school which continued under the missionaries who followed. The band welcomed this opportunity for education. In 1906 they cut and freighted logs for a school building, and received from the government as payment, supplies of flour, bacon, tea, sugar, and gunpowder.[9] School enrollment stood at forty-six in 1906 and thirty-eight in 1907.[10]

Between the departure of William Ivens in 1908 and the arrival of Luther Schuetze in 1927, there were nine different teachers at Little Grand. Their wages were paid by the Department of Indian Affairs through the Methodist Church.[11]

In 1912 J.R. Bunn, Inspector of Indian Agencies, wrote that at Little Grand Rapids there was an unplastered log school building fit for summer work only. This building may not have been located on the reserve, since the Anishinabe did not live on their allotted reserve. The Indian agent reported to Indian Affairs in 1917 that every year when he came to Little Grand Rapids to make annuity payments, the Anishinabe asked for a teacher and a small portion of land to be added to the reserve. In 1916 they had begun to construct some log buildings, including a school, outside of the reserve boundaries12 [near the H.B. Co. Post] Perhaps this is why the Methodist Church didn't know where to place their mission on the reserve.

Between 1919 and 1922, Arthur Barner, Superintendent of Evangelism, corresponded with D.C. Scott in Ottawa about the location of the reserve. Barner wrote that the Methodists were planning to "station a missionary" at Little Grand Rapids, who would also serve at Deer Lake and Pikangikum. At present, wrote Barner, the Anishinabe were not living on the reserve, which was located about three miles from the Hudson's Bay Company post. Rather, they lived near the post during the freighting season. Barner's opinion was that the reserve should be located close to the post because the land there was better for gardening purposes, and because the freighters would be closer to home when they landed. Barner wrote: "Our missionary board would not be willing to erect buildings anywhere until it is quite settled as to where the reserve will be and there are good reasons for having the missionary and the school and Hudson's Bay sites as near together as possible. The school building and cemetery are quite near the Hudson's Bay Post."[13]

Apparently Barner didn't get a satisfactory answer, because he inquired about the same matter in April of 1922. A.F. MacKenzie, the Acting Assistant Deputy and Secretary of Indian Affairs, replied that the department could not give any advice because it did not have the necessary information. In August J.D. McLean, Assistant Deputy and Secretary of Indian Affairs, wrote to Barner that he had been at the reserve, had spoken with the Anishinabe, and had found that they lived near the post in summer and hunted during the winter. He indicated that no plans had been made to change the location of the reserve. Barner replied as follows:

I may point out at this juncture that the only building available in which to teach school in that district is situated at Little Grand Rapids, near the Hudson's Bay Post. When Mr. Niddrie, our Missionary, went up there in July, to assist Mr. Hope in erecting a small dwelling, he held council with the Indians regarding the best place to carry on for the present time. With the exception of one man, they decided to conduct school in the church at Little Grand Rapids. Therefore a small house was erected, the walls of logs, in which Mr. Hope will live this year. If it is finally decided that there shall be no change in the location of the Reserve, it may be necessary to change the site for the schoolhouse to one of the other points mentioned in your letter.[14]

In 1922 Mr. Hope conducted school in the church building with twenty children in attendance.[15] In 1924 members of the band, on their own initiative, hauled seventy logs to a site in the centre of the reserve to build a school building 20 by 30 ft., with an addition for a teacher's residence of 12 by 20 feet. The Anishinabe were willing to donate their labour, but the government was to furnish rations, blackboards, books, and stationery. The windows and stove from the old building could be used in the new building. However, the building was not completed in 1925 because of a shortage of materials.

In 1926 Rev. John Niddrie from Berens River ordered and received from the Department of Indian Affairs, for the school children's midday meal, 200 lbs. of beans, 50 lbs. of blue peas, 20 lbs. of cocoa, and 2 cases of evaporated milk. Luther Schuetze continued the practice of ordering food for the children's lunches.

In 1926 the Roman Catholic Church sent Frederick Leach to Little Grand Rapids to start a school. He stayed one year and wrote an interesting account of his experiences, which is contained in Appendix C. In 1928 the Roman Catholics began their own day school at Little Grand Rapids, with Boniface Guimond as the teacher.[16]

A free trader prior to his missionary work, Schuetze had dealt with the Indian people in the inland area along the east side of Lake Winnipeg. He was therefore very familiar with the whole of the Berens River system many years before he went to serve the church at Little Grand Rapids. He was successful, competing with the Hudson's Bay Company which, he claimed, was far too greedy during this period, making it easy for him to set honest and fair prices that allowed both him and the Indian people a good living.[17]

After Luther Schuetze

In 1939 Richard Schuetze succeeded Luther as the lay missionary teacher at Little Grand Rapids. There were 49 families (275 persons) under pastoral care, and church membership stood at 149. From 1940 to 1942, Colin Douglas Street, formerly the Indian day school teacher at Berens River (where he taught Richard Schuetze), came to Little Grand Rapids as a lay missionary teacher. Following Street, three lay missionary teachers from the Mennonite Brethren denomination served between 1943 and 1947. Nicholas Allan Dueck and Abram Neufeld were doing alternate service as conscientious objectors during World War II, and John M. Schmidt served after the war. These Mennonite Brethren performed infant and child baptisms, unusual for Mennonites who practise adult baptism upon confession of faith.[18]

The Nineties

The 1992 United Church of Canada Yearbook states that Little Grand Rapids is in the Keewatin Presbytery, as a member of the All Native Circle Conference. Raymond Eaglestick was ordained in 1982 under Native Ministries and began his ministry at Little Grand Rapids that same year. Now deceased, he was the son of David Eaglestick mentioned in Schuetze's story. David represented the U.C. at Little Grand Rapids before his son succeeded him.

In 1996, while Rev. Raymond Eaglestick was at Little Grand Rapids, there was one place of worship, one school, thirty households under pastoral care, ten financially supporting households, and a total membership of ten, with an average weekly attendance of seventy. Total membership of the church school was forty-nine.[19]

According to an evaluation report of education at Little Grand Rapids,[20] in 1992 there were approximately 170 students from Nursery to Grade 10. The Southeast Tribal Division administered the Little Grand Rapids School for

Schools Inc., which is part of the Southeast Resource Development Council Corporation, an umbrella organization that provides a variety of governance services to nine First Nation reserves. This organization's intent has been to maintain, for each of the schools under its jurisdiction, as much autonomy and self-direction as possible.

The 1992 evaluation, however, shows that all has not been well with Little Grand Rapids education. Student attendance patterns have been irregular. Most students starting high school have dropped out. Between 1987 and 1992, there were only three graduates from Grade 12. Moreover, Provincial Achievement Testing Programs showed low student performance.

This evaluation concludes that the failure of the education system has been largely due to a very high turnover of teachers; some didn't last even one whole school year. In 1992, the principal and eleven out of thirteen teachers were non-natives. Most of the teachers were inexperienced and had no background in cross-cultural education.

According to one teacher, ten out of fourteen teachers who taught at Little Grand Rapids in 1997–98 weren't planning to return the next year.

Aerial photograph of U.C. Mission

Little Grand Rapids has a nursing station, two pool halls and a general store on the reserve. Off the reserve there is a Northern Store, a fishing lodge, and a landing strip for daily flights. The reserve's water supply, from Family Lake, is chlorinated by a small treatment plant and is distributed by a water delivery truck.

The economic base of Little Grand Rapids is fishing, trapping, and seasonal rice harvesting.[21] Aluminum boats with high-powered outboard motors have replaced the canvas-covered canoes on Family Lake in the summer. In winter, snowmobiles replace dog teams and carrioles [sleds]. Cars and trucks now drive to the community on the winter road where horse-drawn sleighs once freighted in supplies.

Electricity and accessibility have brought with them television sets, modern appliances, computers. Some seventy years ago Luther Schuetze journeyed by canoe to Little Grand Rapids—little could he imagine the far different world this piece of "God's vineyard," as he called it, would become.

by Alvina Block and Herman Schuetze

Endnotes to Introduction

1. The *Little Grand Rapids Post Journal* is on microfilm (see Big Fall, B.18/A10) in the Hudson's Bay Company Archives (HBCA) at the Manitoba Archives.

2. Alexander Morris, Letter to the Minister of the Interior, July 12, 1876. On file at the Treaty & Aboriginal Rights Research Centre of Manitoba Inc. (TARR).

3. A.W. Ponton to the Superintendent General of Indian Affairs at Ottawa, 3 November 1888.

4. Sessional Papers (No. 27) A 1905. Part I, p. 123.

5. A. Irving Hallowell, *The Ojibwa of Berens River, Manitoba: Ethnography Into History*, Harcourt Brace College Publishers, 1922, p. 13.

6. Ibid., p. 29.

7. Methodist Church of Canada, Minutes of Annual Conference 1899, p. 360. On file in the United Church Archives (UCA), University of Winnipeg.

8. Susan Elaine Gray, *"The Ojibwa World View and Encounters with Christianity along the Berens River; 1875–1940."* Ph.D. diss., University of Manitoba, 1996, p. 174.

9. Provincial Archives of Manitoba (PAM), RG10, Reel C7962, Vol. 6239, File 523–5.

10. Susan Elaine Gray, op. cit., p. 175, p. 206.

11. Joseph F. Woodsworth replaced Ivens in 1908, followed by Joseph Jones in 1909. Roy Taylor taught at Little Grand Rapids in 1910, J.H. Wilding in 1911, and Alfred G. Johnson in 1914. These teachers taught only in the summer months and were paid three

dollars per teaching day. In 1918 Mary Jane Manakwap was appointed teacher for the summer months and received $300 for her services. W.J. Hope was the teacher in 1922, and Miss Mina Moar, who had a Grade 11 education, taught in 1924 and 1925. John James Everett taught in 1925, 1926, and 1927 at a rate of four dollars per hour. Everett taught during the winter months as well as in summer. (Source: PAM, RG10, Reel C7962, Vol. 6239, File 523-5).

12. Carter, Letter to J.D. McLean, January 30, 1917. On file at TARR.

13. Arthur Barner, Letter to D.C. Scott, April 26, 1919. On file at TARR.

14. Arthur Barner, Letter to Department of Indian Affairs, August 29, 1922. On file at TARR.

15. PAM, RG10, Reel C7962, Vol. 6239, File 532-5.

16. PAM, RG10, Reel C7962, Vol. 6239, File 532-5.

17. R. Brock Saunders, Luther Schuetze at Little Grand Rapids, in Schuetze biographical file, UCA.

18. Other missionaries at Little Grand Rapids between 1951 and 1960 were S.R. Hale, Clinton Robertson, Glen W. Thompson and Gordon M. Craig.

19. The United Church of Canada Yearbook and Directory, 1996. On file at UCA.

20. Kangas & Associates, Phase 1 Evaluation Report: Little Grand Rapids First Nations, 1992.

21. First Nations Community Profiles 1995—Manitoba Region, Indian and Northern Affairs Canada.

Reverend L.L. Schuetze on his retirement, 1964

Prologue

After eleven years as missionaries in Little Grand Rapids, Manitoba, we were transferred to Berens River, Manitoba. It was there that the late Dr. R.B. Cochrane, Secretary of Home Missions, visited us in the beginning of the 1940s, and sowed the first seed of the work you are about to read. He had heard of our wonderful experiences among the natives of Little Grand Rapids, and he wanted me to write a book about it! I smilingly told him that there never was time enough for anyone to write if he was earnestly engaged wholeheartedly as a missionary among the native peoples. Dr. Cochrane then confronted my wife, and told her to make certain that I'd write this book. As a wonderful, understanding helpmate given me straight from God, she never tried to persuade me, knowing full well that there was no time.

So the years passed by until my active ministry here in Penticton, when I was privileged to address a group of men in a retreat at Naramata, during the afternoon as well as in the evening. At the close, gathering by the fireplace, the flames giving the only illumination, Dr. William Rose stood up and said: "The church should give this man a year off and get him to write a book about his experiences."

That was over a year ago. Having had several attacks of angina, I was advised by our doctor to give up the active ministry of the Church. This I did, and after taking a prolonged holiday at Bella Coola and the Cariboo, I feel much better. I am now confronted with the decision somehow to record part of our life as a witness to the wonderful living reality of Christ's dealing with us and through us, and thus perhaps be the means of helping others in various ways to find their faith and have it strengthened. You see, I am retired now, but living among the people whom I served these last three years, and I still find many needs to be supplied. However, this burden of writing seems to have been laid upon me.

Luther L. Schuetze

Penticton, BC, January 4, 1964

1

I OWED MY LIFE TO HIM

1891 to 1926

A Christian Mother's Song

Everything has a beginning, somewhere. My physical existence began in Joinville, Brazil, on March 17, 1891. Awareness of real life perhaps began with one German song my mother used to sing to me when I was a wee chap. Her voice, when she sang me to sleep in times of illness, seemed sweeter than an angel, and some of the words still linger:

> How could I peacefully fall asleep in the darkest night?
> If I had not first thought of Thee, my God and Father.
> The distractions of the day disturbed my heart.
> With Thee, with Thee alone is peace and soul's delight.[1]

Perhaps not quite correct, but nevertheless it is still there after over sixty years, proof of a Christian mother's great influence over the lives of her little ones.

The Miracle

After finishing school in Brazil, I studied three years in Germany,[2] then joined my family who had moved to Canada. In Northern Alberta, on a bed of poles and hay, my life-changing experiences began. I had taken up homesteading after the family farm near Winnipeg was sold, and there I lay in a one-room log cabin—deathly sick with typhoid fever, double pneumonia, and another disease, the name of which I have forgotten.

The kind neighbours drove thirty-five miles through the December snow to get a doctor. Later they told me I had been unconscious for six weeks, and that the women who nursed me had to raise me up to let the blood from my lungs run out of my mouth. They kept me alive by feeding me spoonfuls of egg white and brandy.

One day a stranger came in, whom no one knew, and asked if he could pray for me. The lady who was looking after me at first refused. Then when she looked at me, it seemed to her that I wanted this. I could not talk, but must

Rodi, Luther, and their father Eugen at the farm, c. 1906

Luther, Eugen, and Rodi canoeing into the Manitoba bush country, c. 1914

have had a conscious moment, for I remember the stranger kneeling there, that is all.

Now comes the strange part: I couldn't speak, I couldn't move, but I could hear. The doctor must have had suspicions of this on his last visit, for he took the lady outside the door, and I heard him say he would come again in the morning to make out the death certificate. The door was made of single plain boards, and my bed's headrest was right next to it.

This must have startled me, yet I cannot remember any sense of fear. However, a great feeling of remorse overcame me as I became enveloped in complete darkness. Then I saw my life to that point as complete selfishness, without much regard for others.

At that moment, I prayed in my heart, for I couldn't speak, and at once the living image of Christ appeared before me, not at all as I used to see Him in pictures, but tall, dark, and gloriously beautiful. My prayer was: "Lord, give me another chance."

And He said: "Thou shalt live; sin no more."

In the morning when the doctor came, I was fully conscious. I made such rapid progress toward restored health that, when I visited him later in regard to my account, he said, "If ever I have just one of the diseases you have had, and would be in a hospital and had the best of care, I still would call myself fortunate to get well as quickly as you did. This was a miracle."

Near the end of March all the snow had gone before a Chinook wind, except for a great pile of red-stained snow, a grim reminder of all the blood I had coughed up. I knew I now owed my life to Him who loved me and gave Himself for me. Gone were the days when I forgot about religious exercises and tried to still the inner hunger with the study of philosophical works of authors such as Schopenhauer and Nietzsche; the days when working to exhaustion late at night and rising early seemed to be the only real satisfaction of life. From that miraculous time on, life had a new perspective, a new purpose. I had a new assurance and awareness of the needs of others, and also a yearning for the companionship of others who loved the Lord.

Seattle

In the meantime, my parents moved to Seattle, and there I found companionship among Christ-centred young people. I used to visit the penitentiary with them. We would go in, two pairs of young men and women. We sang hymns and gave our testimony of what our Christian faith meant to us. Years later a sign painter in Castle Rock, Washington, recognized me and asked me how much the government paid us for coming to the penitentiary, of which he was an inmate at the time.

"Nothing," I said. "We came because we wanted to help you, and tell you how much our Christ-faith meant to us."

He replied, "My, that must be wonderful to feel like that."

And it is.

Marriage

In Castle Rock the Lord gave me a helpmate—Augusta (Gusti) Hoffman. We were married on August 20, 1921, for which I am still thankful to Him after forty-three

Gusti at Poplar River, c. 1925

years of married life. I told my wife of the northland in Manitoba, and she wanted to see it.

So after our wedding we took off for Saskatoon and I took a job at Macklin on a big farm, running a separator in threshing time. The owner was so pleased with our service that he paid me twelve dollars a day and my board, and Augusta, two dollars a day for helping his wife in the kitchen.

Soon we had a stake to go out. I ordered a canoe, tent, guns, ammunition, traps, groceries, etc., and when threshing was over we took off for Berens River on Lake Winnipeg, where our outfit awaited us.

We went by canoe up the Pigeon River, and with the help of my brother Rodi (Roderick), who had preceded us, built a nice, cozy, comfortable cabin near Round Lake. Then Rodi built his own camp about ten miles farther up. There we wintered, making one trip out to Berens River for Christmas, where Gusti was treated like a queen, being the only white woman at that time. She was taken home by dog team, comfortably covered in a carriole, by Jimmy McKay and his man Arthur Shavanass, a two or three-day trip of about eighty miles.

All this was a preparation for the life that was about to come. As we look back now, we can easily see the hand of God and His infinite wisdom and goodness leading us to our destiny. In my heart I knew I had to serve Him. I thought of faraway fields—China, etc.— however, we were led differently.

Carriole on a bay of Lake Winnipeg near the Poplar River Trading Post

Ralph's Birth

The following year [1922], our first-born son, Ralph, arrived in Winnipeg at the end of May. However, we were drawn back up north and finally established ourselves at Poplar River. There we built a general store, a warehouse, and a home with a garden for ourselves. We had a 40-foot boat, formerly a sailboat, which we converted into a motor boat by installing a car engine. We also had the post office and mail contract, and established another trading post about 150 miles inland. My father, Carl Eugen Felix Schuetze, came to stay with us. It was a challenging, interesting life, travelling by canoe in summer and by dogs and snowshoes in the winter, going far into the interior, taking thousands of dollars worth of furs to Winnipeg and auctioning them off. Now, all this is but preliminary to our story, leading up to our missionary work among the Saulteaux Indians [Anishinabe] in the interior.

2

THE TRADER LEAVES HOME
1926

At Poplar River

My work began this way. One day in 1926, two men walked into our store at Poplar River. One was Dr. Arthur Barner, Superintendent of Indian Missions, out from United Church headquarters in Toronto, and the other was the Rev. John Niddrie,[3] minister of the Berens River church. They had come up to visit the Poplar River Mission, where the Rev. William Lee was ministering. Our store was about two miles from the mission, and the only way to it in summer was by boat. We had never met Dr. Barner, and had only seen Rev. Niddrie once.

Without much ado, they asked me point blank if I would be willing to build a mission for the United Church in Little Grand Rapids.

I knew the place. It was 108 miles up the Berens River, and you had to negotiate 50-odd rapids and falls. A perilous and hard road.

All at once a feeling that is hard to describe made me tongue-tied. Then, after a deep breath, I asked them how on earth they got this idea. I was a prosperous trader at the time, had built up a fine business, and here two strange men came in and asked me to give it all up! Dr. Barner explained that the Rev. William Lee had highly recommended me. Still I could not see how they got the idea.

Then Mr. Niddrie spoke up. "Last summer," he said, "we had an outdoor meeting on the Berens River Reserve at Chief William Berens's place. You stood apart from us near the riverbank."

"That is right," I said, "I remember."

"Well," he continued, "while I was praying I asked the Lord, as I have for a long time, to send someone up to Little Grand Rapids, and when I looked up there you were, and the Lord as much as said to me: There is your man."

Hearing these words, I knew this was it. But there were many other voices: It is impossible! What about your family?

So I asked if there was a comfortable place for my family. We had three boys by this time, and another on the way.

From left: C.D. Street, Mike Elias and Reverend John Niddrie

Mr. Niddrie assured me there was. So I answered, "Well, then I will pray about it, and see what I can do."

My father, a former chartered accountant, was keeping books for me and no storekeeper ever had it so good. I always knew exactly where I stood. My credit in Winnipeg was so good that I always had to take care I would not expand too rapidly and too much.

So I decided to entreat my brother Rodi, who was trapping in the interior with his wife, to take over without any obligations whatsoever. "No, I am not interested," was his reply.

That year I had bought one of the first radios, a peanut tube set. When I made my trips to the interior with the dogs, I always travelled alone, as I never could find satisfactory partners for long and dangerous trips like these. The following December I took the radio along and arrived at my brother's camp on Christmas Eve. We put up the antenna, and all the lovely Christmas music came in. It was really something to hear this far in the wilderness. Now I thought

Poplar River Trading Post and beach; Toni, Rodi and son in foreground

Rodi's heart would be softened, but again he said no. On my return journey several days later, I called at his place and tried one more time, but the answer was still No!

I prayed some more and waited some more. Well, that winter Rodi caught nothing to any amount, which was unusual, since he was a very successful trapper. When he came out of the bush, my prayers were answered. "I'll take it," he told me. Our father would stay with him and take care of the store and bookkeeping.

So it happened on an August morning in the year of our Lord 1927, a heavily loaded canoe left the sheltered bay of our home, the home we had hewed out of the wilderness in the previous years. The canoe held all that was most dear to us: our adopted son Richard, thirteen years old,[4] Rolf (Ralph), five, Herman, four, Ernie, two, and Albert, seven months old. We also took along two of our best sleigh dogs. Turning the point in the Poplar River, we waved good-bye to my father, Rodi, and his wife and son, never to set foot again upon this lovely spot.

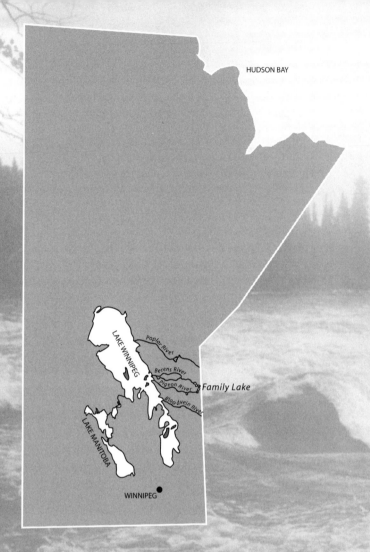

HUDSON BAY

LAKE WINNIPEG

Poplar River

Betens River

Pigeon River

Family Lake

Bloodvein River

LAKE MANITOBA

WINNIPEG

3

THROUGH DANGEROUS WATERS
WITH OUR LORD
1927

Leaving Poplar River

Our two-horsepower Evinrude steadily pushed us out into Lake Winnipeg (which is about eighty miles across at the mouth of Poplar River) and then southerly to Berens River, about seventy miles away.

Berens River, once mentioned in the government tourist booklet as the "Garden of Manitoba," has a beauty of its own. The evergreens and granite islets made us feel as if we had already partly arrived. The river itself originates in Ontario, and its brownish waters are easily discernible as they embrace the muddy water of Lake Winnipeg.

We seemed so vulnerable, so helpless, and so small. Skirting the many reefs, we sometimes had to stay quite a distance out in the lake. Lake Winnipeg can whip up quite a storm in a short time, but we were fortunate, as we reached Berens River safely that day.

Somehow we knew and felt that this was the beginning of our real destiny, and that the Lord of Hosts was with us all the way.

Falls and Portages

After a brief visit with the Rev. John Niddrie and his housekeeper niece, Miss Annie Niddrie, we were on

Freighting on the Berens River: Luther Schuetze, Fred Whiteway, and Karl Hoffman (Augusta's brother)

Opposite: Little Grand Rapids

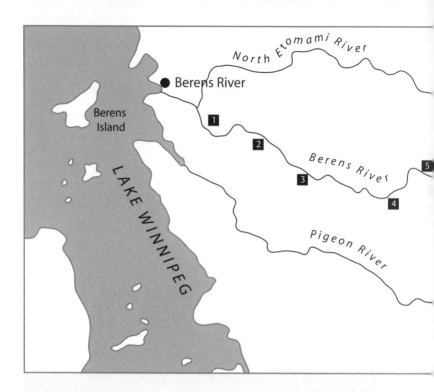

Portaging on the Berens River

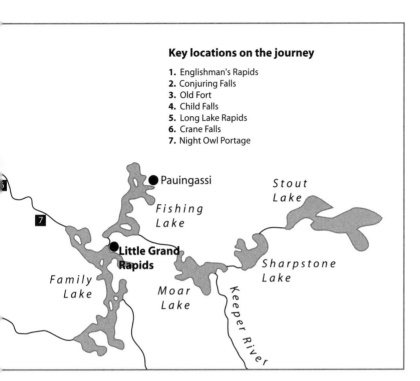

Key locations on the journey

1. Englishman's Rapids
2. Conjuring Falls
3. Old Fort
4. Child Falls
5. Long Lake Rapids
6. Crane Falls
7. Night Owl Portage

Pauingassi

Stout Lake

Fishing Lake

Little Grand Rapids

Sharpstone Lake

Family Lake

Moar Lake

Keeper River

Route from Berens River to Family Lake

our way. Somewhere around 50 rapids and falls, and 108 tortuous miles of portages and swift currents, lay ahead of us.

However, we knew every current in that river, having freighted up it many times as a means of livelihood, and with a love for adventure and daring challenge. But never before with active boys who had to be watched every minute, for in many places one misstep meant death in the swirling, thundering waters. And so Gusti had a job and a half on her hands, for I had to see that canoe and freight surmounted the currents and got across the portages.

Nevertheless, it was an eerie feeling to start out thus into the unknown, and it was a good thing we did not know what lay ahead of us in the years to come, for it could have daunted us and made us hesitate. Here we were, a small, frail craft propelled by a two-horsepower outboard motor, pitting ourselves against the power of the onrushing waters, so mighty we often could hear the falls long before we reached them. However, we were fully aware of the presence of our Lord who promised His ever-presence to all who believed in Him, and we were content.

Making good progress, we soon came to the first challenge—Englishman's Rapid—apparently so named after a fatal accident there. We had to land and portage across a small bare rock point. The whole rock formation along this river is granite, as is the whole east side of Lake Winnipeg (the west side is limestone).

So the first step had been taken, and away we were again, soon to hear the thunder of the Sturgeon Falls. There are two of them, one above the other, making two steep portages necessary. Here we had to use our pack-straps: a wide leather band for the forehead, and long thongs to tie in the freight. We were accustomed to this, as our average load used to be three hundred pounds.

This is an art, or used to be, as the river was the only lifeline for many natives in the hinterland and the various trading posts. The native boys learned this early, but many white men never really got the hang of it. I have seen small native men making their way across the portage with 400 pounds, the man weighing about 150 pounds, and alongside him a hulking white man hardly able to get across with 200 pounds. Our youngsters enjoyed the portages tremendously, were always hungry and thirsty, and constantly had to be watched.

Island Falls were next, and the portage not so long and difficult. Then the long portage of the Wolverine Rapids, and right around the corner, Grey Willow Falls, which presented a lovely picture and a fair portage. Next came Kettle Rapids, followed in swift order by the Net Rapids and Little and Big Conjuring Rapids, all necessitating portages.

Big Conjuring Falls is quite a long portage, about three or four hundred yards. Then we had a good long run of about one hour, seeing the odd blue heron walking along the shore picking up his meal, the kingfisher making quite a noise as though he resented our disturbing the quiet peacefulness of the river's gently flowing waters. Moose Dung Portage was another long one, with a bit of a climb, but on the other side we again had a long run of nearly an hour. This brought us to the Old Fort, the first portage on a sidearm, which was almost dry and presented no danger for the children.

It now being evening, we put up our family mosquito bar, which we had manufactured ourselves. It was a cottage roof-type top of English ticking, waterproofed with alum and sugar of lead. The sides were mosquito netting. In the meantime, Gusti had prepared supper, and after giving thanks to our Father in Heaven for having brought us safely so far, we all went to bed and had a good night's rest.

The next morning our boys saw to it that we got a good, early start. There was so much excitement—so many things to see! It was nice to be together thus, out among God's creation, away from the bickering and trivialities of men. One felt so peaceful, so rested, and so fresh. And with it all, a deep sense of gratitude for all God's wonderful goodness.

There was a series of three portages for the Old Fort—then we were away to Stepping over the Stick. It was a dangerous place for the kiddies, and they hung close to their mother's skirts. The rapids and falls now came thick and fast: White Mud Rapids, a fairly long and safe portage; Sharp Rock Falls, another dangerous spot for the children; then the Queen's

Queen's Chair rock formation

Chair and its small rapid, and above it, the lovely White Beaver Falls, a thundering cascade of whiteness.

A short trip and already a whole series of falls and rapids! I called the next one Rodi's Falls, for it was here some years before that my brother had been swept over. I'd managed to get below the falls and grab him. Then came the Flat Rock Rapids, Gaminigate Rapids, Ghost Rapids, Pine Island Falls, Sideway Portage, and Child Falls, where a native woman gave birth and the very next morning was in the icy waters helping to pull up the canoe! The child grew into a vigorous, stout man.

The Crooked Current is a deceptive rapid in which many men had been drowned and articles of freight lost. The current was very strong without appearing so, whirling sideways and catching one unawares. The portage is fairly long, with a climb to it. Here we camped a safe distance away from the dangerous waters.

From this point on we had only three short portages— Wolf Rapids, Creek Rapids, and Long Lake Rapids. Here we stopped a while and examined the holes drilled straight down in solid granite as with a mighty augur. They were two or three feet wide, and one of them over two feet deep. This must have happened aeons ago, and always at the bottom of each hole was a stone that must have been whirled around and around, until finally the waters receded and it stopped. One of the wonders of nature.

On Long Lake we had a good rest until we came to Little Moose Rapids, and then Moose Painted Stone where, above the falls on the north side of the high granite walls, someone ages ago had painted a moose, no doubt with red ochre paint. Here the natives always make an oblation to the water gods for a safe journey.

Antoine Rapids, Manitou Rapids, Crane Falls were next—and then White Man's Rapid where I almost met my end, years later. At that time I was taking the treaty party around, and we had camped on an island where the rapids ran on either side. In the middle of the night I was awakened out of a deep sleep. It was Mr. Millidge, the clerk, telling me,

"Luther, Luther, Hector is walking near the rapids." Well, the Indian Agent had the D.T.'s, and sure enough, there he was, walking near the edge on top of the rapids, waving across in the dim light and calling, "Hello little bird, hello little bird."

I was walking on the outside of him, right on the very edge, when all at once he gave me a shove, saying, "You want to go in?"

Well, I pretty near went, and would've been the second white man drowned there. The natives say that long ago a Hudson's Bay man, taking a canoe and running from some natives, tried to shoot the rapids, flipped over, and drowned. Hence, it became known as White Man's Rapid.

From there, our family had only one more obstacle in our way, and that was the Owl Portage. I imagine it's close to a half mile long. After this we were on Family Lake, and had only a little more than an hour ahead of us before arriving at Little Grand Rapids and our destiny.

Arrival at Little Grand Rapids

We landed at the shore of the reserve where our house and the school were supposed to be. Soon dozens of people had gathered around us. After unloading, we carried our belongings up to the building site. Our hearts sank when we saw the house. Built of logs chinked with moss, it was only about ten by twelve feet. The roof was constructed out of poles maybe three inches wide, with tarpaper tacked on top. And here we were, a family of seven! And it was late toward fall, with school starting the beginning of September. We tried, but could not get someone to work for us and build another house [on an island off-shore from the reserve], so we got to work right away ourselves, and built on a lean-to for our bedrooms.

Gusti by the first house with our addition and the doghouse Richard built, 1927

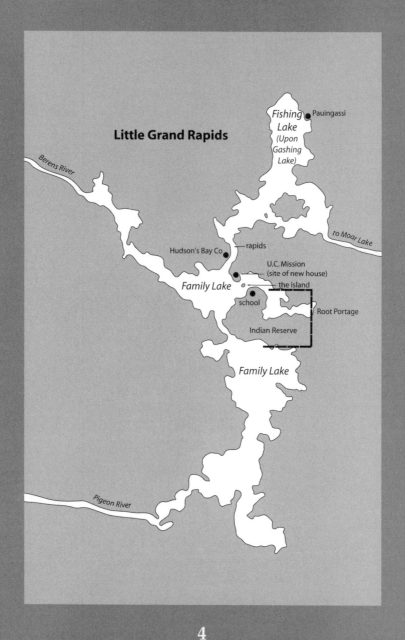

Little Grand Rapids

Berens River

Fishing Lake
(Upon Gashing Lake)

Pauingassi

to Moar Lake

rapids

Hudson's Bay Co

U.C. Mission
(site of new house)

the island

Family Lake

school

Root Portage

Indian Reserve

Family Lake

Pigeon River

4

A LONG-NEGLECTED VINEYARD
1927 to 1928

Ministering to the Sick

I believe it was the first night, while we were all sound asleep, that the chief's son, Pemuchicak, came over and wanted us right away—his mother had a terrible toothache. Luckily I had some of my father's dental equipment with me—forceps, iodine, and cotton batting. I walked back with the lad to his home not so very far away.

There was no light in the house except a flickering candle. The chief's wife, a large woman, was lying down and groaning. I got her to sit on a box, had the boy hold up the candle to give me light, and with a silent prayer, took hold of a great molar with a cavity and yanked it out. I had studied and learned a good deal about this, but still was not too sure of myself. I guess I was more relieved than the chief's wife. When I looked at the tooth, I saw between its roots a bit of lamella of the jawbone. Here already, in the beginning, we felt the reality of our Lord's presence, and His answer to prayer fulfilled. The more we look back, the surer we become of this glorious fact, so often lost because of our unbelief and lack of faith.

Chief Alex Boucher and some of his family: Shoomai (back right); Stanley, Boniface, and the Chief's wife (front)

Well here we were, trying to make our family comfortable for the oncoming winter, and right away becoming aware that this was a long-neglected vineyard of our Lord.

Handsawing lumber

The very next day we were called to a tent where a boy all covered with flies was experiencing convulsions. An awful picture to behold and not forgotten to this day. We thought how the churches were clamouring for missionaries for faraway lands while our native peoples, like Lazarus, are lying right at our door. There is not much glamour attached to this type of work, but there is an inner satisfaction of working with God that nothing else can supersede.

Inadequate Facilities

Gusti was afraid that the house, being heated only with airtight heaters,[5] would be too cold for Albert, our little one, only about eight months old. She wanted to know if she could cut off a piece of my eiderdown robe, which we had made ourselves from English ticking and ten pounds of pure goose down. It broke my heart, but I, too, was afraid, for we could see right through our house, and the floor was only one-ply, hand-sawn boards with wide cracks between.

There were troubles and problems everywhere. The school, too, was a problem—the roof, just tarpaper nailed on poles; the floor, big cracks; and the only facilities for the pupils, seating of hewn logs with four wooden legs, and a blackboard made from cloth nailed on logs.

Our church services were also to be held in the school. Just imagine sitting for worship on a log when a rainstorm comes up, the place leaks like a sieve, and you must scramble to find a log on the other side! So this was to be our place of operation, and there wasn't much we could do about it at the present. [Later that year, Schuetze ordered lumber for tables and benches.]

School Begins

When school started, we went around with our canoe and picked up all the children whose parents lived on islands or across the other side [a distance of about two miles each way]. I had widened the canoe (a Chestnut "freighter") considerably for this purpose, especially at the stern, and we often carried more than twenty. Our faithful old outboard never failed us, no matter how windy the weather. Gas was expensive up here, $3 a gallon, the same as coal oil. However, we had a good school attendance all the time.

In the beginning, I thought I would lose my students, for I discovered they were covered with vermin. So I took my hair clippers and some insect powder, and cut their hair clean off. I had no trouble, because the children were eager to come to school.

Then I found out something that hurt me deep inside. The Indian Department furnished biscuits for the school children, and I was allowed to give each of them two for lunch. Well, the very first time, I believe, I saw a little girl eating one biscuit and putting one away in her blouse. I asked her through an interpreter what she was going to do with that biscuit.

She told me, "I am taking it home for my little brother. He is hungry too!"

After this I got busy, and in all the years I taught in Little Grand Rapids, I saw to it that these children, besides their two biscuits, got a cup of hot cocoa and a warm meal. I furnished this myself until I appealed to the Indian Department, who then sent me ample supplies of rice, beans, milk, and cocoa. We gave the children a change during the winter, serving whitefish and potatoes. We had cleared a goodly piece of land and grew lovely vegetables, and I always hung up somewhere around two thousand whitefish, ten to a stick, averaging about four pounds. These the children loved best of all.[6]

So far so good, but how to teach children who could not speak a word of English, and I couldn't speak a word of their native tongue. I had the curriculum, and all the needs and standards of education. Here I prayed again, and the problem was soon solved, for the children and I quickly learned one another's language. When I tested them (some had had teachers before), they could rattle off the ABCs, but when I wrote the letters on the blackboard, they didn't know one from the other. Well, the inspiration came! I drew a leaf on the blackboard.

Right away I heard here and there: Nibishun.

Then above it I printed the letters "L E A F." Very soon they all said leaf, and we were away. I soon became the official interpreter for the Mounted Police, the Indian Agent, and the Air Force. So far I'd had to depend on the Hudson's Bay for my interpreter on Sunday services. Later on, the church would send me James Kirkness to assist with interpreting. My class in school always numbered more than forty. Among them I had, at first, Rolf, Herman, and some of the trader Joe Alix's children. [An attendance of 40 was high compared with previous years. In 1922 Mr. Hope had an average of 20 children.[15]]

Relocating the Mission

In the spring I decided the reserve was not a good place for the mission, so I chose a point one mile across the lake [see map, page 48]. It was handy to everyone, and a lovely spot. It had a nice sandy beach in the bay, very good fishing, and lovely soil for gardens. I had some logs cut and freighted them over. With the help of my son Richard and Mr. Colin Douglas Street (the Berens River schoolteacher), I cut a line right across the point, claiming this land for the United Church. Soon after I sent in the description, the Hudson's Bay Company, which had been there about fifty years, saw the advantage of our situation and wanted to trade us. However, we shrugged it off.

When we visited Little Grand Rapids in 1960, we found that the church had lost almost everything through no one caring for or looking after the place. The church building

Gusti and children looking over the new mission site

was still standing, but was used for storing Indian Department lumber. The natives had pulled the manse down, and the Hudson's Bay Company had moved over, partly on the land we claimed. The "line" was all grown up now, and the church had re-established itself on the reserve. There were other changes, as well. The Indian Department

Luther Schuetze returns to his church, 1960

had built a four-bed hospital. The Forestry had constructed a dock and a building near the beach, and erected a tower further up. During the last war, many of our missions were unmanned because of the scarcity of labourers in the Lord's vineyard.

In the spring of 1928 we moved across on the ice and put up the big tent loaned to us by Johnnie Moar [Hudson's Bay Company manager], always a great friend. I would get up early in the morning, around five, and start clearing the land. Here I must also mention an incident I've never forgotten. While I was busy grubbing out stumps, I heard a noise—and there was little Herman, about four-and-a-half, grunting and rolling off a stump. Herman, now six-foot-six, as always remains the same, ever helpful on any occasion.

After breakfast I'd get off to school. When the ice was gone again, we would pick up the children with the canoe, which they called Nsuatese, the Turtle. Only once did we have trouble, when Moose Boucher didn't want to go that day and hid on the island. His parents were concerned, so I gave the high sign to the other kids and they formed a chain, more or less, and cornered the boy. He came quite willingly, and later on proved himself a good worker any time I wanted him.

That same spring we got all our logs, most of them cut a long ways away and hauled home with the canoe and outboard.

Gusti Visits Her Parents

That summer of 1928, Gusti, not having seen her parents for seven years (now moved back to the farm in Alberta), visited them with our four little boys. Frances Moar, the Hudson's Bay manager's daughter, accompanied her as a help with the children. I took them down to Berens River by canoe and saw them off on the S.S. Wolverine, the steamer that made a weekly round trip from Winnipeg to Warren's Landing [with stops at Berens River], where passengers boarded a smaller boat to reach Norway House, a point of historic interest.

Here an incident happened which I have never forgotten. Looking up from my canoe, I saw my little family high up on the deck of the steamer. I waved and said good-bye, and everyone waved back except wee Albert, who let out a mournful howl. He didn't like to see his Daddy leave him!

Making Hay, Putting up Buildings

Soon it was back to work again—finishing the house, clearing more brush, making more garden, and, most important of all, making hay. This was not as simple as it looked, for there wasn't hay ground anywhere near, only miles away, here and there, by a little lake or the mouth of a creek leading into it. The Old Fort just across our lake was the nearest. So we gathered a crew, none of whom had ever handled a scythe, except for a Frenchman named Joe Potvin. Most of us soon became experts, but it wasn't easy with all the old dead grass on the bottom from which untold numbers of flies angrily attacked us when we disturbed their home. Also hidden under the old grass were muskrat channels and holes. Taking a swing with the scythe, one often found oneself up to the knees in a hole from which it was sometimes hard to extricate oneself.

Making hay with Joe Potvin (far right)

The summer of 1928 was also busy with building—the house, barns for the goats and horses, a warehouse for our groceries. Each year we freighted up twenty-four 100-pound sacks of flour. Every month Gusti baked 200 pounds into lovely bread, one of the main staple foods for the boys. We also built a warehouse [in later years] for the Indian Department "Destitute" supplies, which formerly were handled by the Hudson's Bay Company, and had been handed over to us. We were really busy!

Stitching Gordon Moar's Foot

One day while I was plastering the house, Frances Moar came rushing over all out of breath and said, "Mr. Schuetze, they want you right away quick at the Hudson's Bay grounds. Gordon Moar has cut his foot very badly."

I cleaned my hands, grabbed my surgical kit and whatever first aid supplies I had, jumped into my canoe with son Herman in the bow, and rushed over. A great crowd had gathered around a tent near the shore, and here Gordon was lying on a blanket, his foot covered in blood. Closer examination revealed that the Achilles tendon had been severed from the bone. The ends were sticking out, and here I was, never having sewn a stitch nor even seen it done.

The Mission Point in later years

For a moment I stood and prayed in my heart, somewhat like this: "Lord, You have brought me to this; You will have to help me."

And He did. While the mother held her son's head in her lap and wiped away the sweat from his forehead, I selected a length of catgut (it looked like a violin string), for I knew this would have to stay, as I had to sew the wound shut afterward. I cleansed the wound with a disinfectant, then without any sedative, drew the severed tendon together. It had to be drawn tight so it could knit again. I had no assistant except, of course, the Lord.

After the tendon fitted perfectly, I began to put in the stitches to close up the wound. I was about to put in the last stitch when I heard a voice saying, "Leave this open for drainage."

I advised the young man and his mother that this leg must not be used at all, and to keep it perfectly quiet. The next year Gordon Moar was playing football without a limp of any kind. His leg had healed perfectly.

5

SANTA WORE RABBIT SKINS

1928 to 1929

Kittigas's Lead Poisoning and the Medicine Man

In the fall of 1928 we moved into our new house—so far only one big room (about 26 by 40 ft.) with an upstairs for the boys' sleeping quarters. Quite a change from the tent and from the crude little log house. However, we were never certain when we would be tested again!

It was that same winter we were called over to the trading post looked after by Kittigas, one of the natives of Little Grand, for Mike Elias of Bloodvein River. When I entered the room, I found a large crowd. At the end stood a big beribboned drum, and along one side squatted seven medicine men, each with a present such as a shirt, lying on the floor before him. Kittigas lay in a bed opposite, his wife sitting beside him on a chair. He looked very pale and was breathing fast. I noticed several kettles sitting on the floor, and another containing bark of some kind was steaming on the stove.

I examined the patient thoroughly—temperature, pulse. I also had a stethoscope. I looked at his legs; they were swollen considerably. Then I said (through Johnnie Moar, who was interpreting) that I would get some medicine, provided the whole room was cleared and the drum taken out, too, for the man needed absolute quiet. When I came back it was so, but Johnnie told me that the head medicine man, Kittigas's father-in-law, had made an awful row and at first had refused to leave. Then I told Kittigas, through Johnnie, that I was pretty helpless, that only God could save him, that I would pray, and that he'd better pray, too.

Kittigas did recover. This was our first real big victory, because the medicine men had done their best and failed. Recognizing failure, they had called me in, and from then on the power of darkness was on the wane in Little Grand Rapids.

But the struggle still went on. I had recognized Kittigas's trouble as lead poisoning, and found out later that the head conjurer, Machkojence, was making home brew with lead pipes in the still. Other men had died with the same symptoms. So I

Our new house: Gusti holding Daniel; (left to right) Herman, Ernest, Albert, Rolf, Richard (at the back), summer of 1929

59

Kittigas; copy of photograph captioned *Kitegas* by A. Irving Hallowell, courtesy of American Philosophical Society

confronted Machkojence (John Duck) about his home brew-making. Johnnie Moar later confessed that he did not interpret all I had said, for the old man could get really wild, his main objection being that the natives never made intoxicating drinks before the white man came, since it was the white man who taught them how.

Sometimes we were called out in the middle of the night if a baby was restless and crying. I remember that at first the parents wouldn't let me give an enema if the problem was constipation. They were deadly afraid of enemas, but it was not long before they all used them in times of need.

Christmas

Our first Christmas tree in the schoolhouse must be mentioned. It was quite an occasion! The tree was gaily decorated with tinsel and lighted candles and made quite an impression. But I made a mistake by telling the people that Santa Claus would be coming. They didn't know what I meant, so I explained, "A stranger is coming with some presents for the children."

They were deadly afraid of strangers and had the weirdest stories about windigoes (cannibals) who killed and ate native peoples. It seemed every year someone saw a stranger somewhere who was thought to be a windigo, and everyone would pack up and move to another island. So when I said stranger through the interpreter, of course they all became uneasy.

Well, we had dressed up the ranger from Eagle Lake as Santa Claus (we used rabbit skins for the white whiskers), and I told the people the stranger would come with the sound of bells. I have never seen anything like what happened when the bells jingled and the door opened. The whole congregation disappeared under the benches! Some of the women were very stout; how they did it, I don't know. It took a while to assure everyone that the stranger came every year at the time Christ was born, to bring gifts and spread kindness, goodwill, and love amongst the people.

Christmas in succeeding years was much better. I notified Eaton's, the Hudson's Bay, and the Tribune Empty Stocking Fund of the poverty of our people, and a plane came loaded with gifts. Wings Limited freighted in the whole load, gratis, as a Christmas present. It warmed our hearts.

Richard Goes to Berens River

After Christmas the second winter, we decided to take Richard to Mr. Street's school in Berens River to further his education and prepare for university entrance. In all our years we have never met a teacher so dedicated as Colin Douglas Street. His was only a one-room Indian day-school, but he took in every white or native child who wanted to learn, and saw them through to university entrance. Richard was one of the few who availed themselves of this opportunity. When he attended Wesley College in Winnipeg, his grades were always between 90 and a 100. Street was a wonderful Christian teacher who certainly left his mark in the hearts and minds of many.

We hitched up our two dogs and took off for Berens River. The river route was hardly used at that time in the winter. Some had tried and got lost, for the waters were very treacherous, and the country surrounding very rough. Most of the people took the way around to Bloodvein, then north to Berens River, a distance of about 145 miles. We did quite well, Richard and I. The first day we made half of the 108 miles, and the next morning we started early, the dogs pulling our bedding, grub, and Richard's belongings.

That morning it was still a bit dark, the temperatures down below zero. I was looking after the sleigh, Richard running ahead, when I tripped and wrenched my ankle on a root. It was a very bad pain, but nothing was broken, so I hobbled along with excruciating pain, all the time visualizing my arrival in Berens River and getting my foot into hot water.

We arrived at the mission quite late. Mr. Niddrie was preparing for the watch night service, and he asked if I would give the message. My vision of hot water vanished, as it was nearly time to go to church after a meal and a clean-up. And so the thought of hot water had a definite influence on my message, which is why I have never forgotten it.

I preached on the text of Revelation 3, regarding the message to the Church of Laodicea: "I know thy works, that thou are neither cold nor hot. I would thou wert cold or hot. So then because thou art lukewarm, and neither hot nor cold, I will spew thee out of my mouth."

After that I did get my hot water foot-bath, and it felt good, so good.

Getting Building Supplies

After a brief rest, I went to town to get lumber and materials to finish the house. The traders had cut out a road of sorts for winter hauling by teams to Bloodvein River on Lake Winnipeg, a distance of eighty miles. With three camps and stables on the way, it was about an eight-day trip. [Schuetze rode down as far as Matheson Island, or maybe even Fisher River, with the mail carrier in his horse-drawn, heated caboose.]

I found out that the freight charge was prohibitive and would cost more than the material itself, so I looked around [in Winnipeg] for a team of horses. Eaton's and other firms used to lay off some of their delivery horses at this time of year, but I couldn't find any. At last I came to Canada Bread

Company, and the stable boss told me that they, too, had laid off all the horses they intended to. I had prayed for this, my last hope.

Right then one of the owners walked in and asked the stable boss why I wanted the horses. When the boss came over and asked, I told him I wanted to build a mission house and a church, but the freight was so prohibitive I couldn't afford it unless I bought a team of horses and freighted the material in myself. The owner told the boss to take me up to Elmwood and show me Bob and Princess. We found them hitched to a bread wagon and tied only to a strap and weight. They were hackneys, the mare imported from Scotland. Bob was eight years old and Princess was nine. After we drove them around, the boss asked how I liked them. "Fine," I answered, "but they are too expensive for my pocketbook." I had just found out the price for a team of hackneys was five hundred dollars.

When we got back to the barn, the owner (I'm sorry I've forgotten his name, for I owe him a great debt of gratitude) asked how I liked the team.

"Just wonderful, but too high priced for me," I repeated.

"Would $125 dollars be too much?"

I almost fainted, and could only stammer my thanks. Then he told the stable boss to give me their collars, too.

This surely was another clear answer to prayer. Now I could load all the building material, hay, feed, and "Hermona," a purebred Saanen nanny goat who became the foundation of our splendid herd of twenty goats. Their milk was a great help to us as well as to many native mothers who were tubercular and nursing babies who otherwise wouldn't have grown up fine, healthy, and strong.

At Fisher River, then the end of the railroad, I hired two more teams to haul our freight to Bloodvein, about sixty-five miles. In Bloodvein we had to unload a great deal of our lumber, for ahead of us lay eighty miles of very difficult and rough road which would take four days. On the last day, nearly home, a crate of thirty dozen eggs, which were very, very scarce in Little Grand, and which I had purchased in

Fisher River as the weather was quite mild, fell off the sleigh. Many eggs were broken—too good to throw away, impossible to take along. One chap [Luther] suggested we eat them, so we sucked away. I believe I downed thirty of them without any bad after-effects.

The next day the two Fisher River teams went home after being paid off, and a few days later I returned to Bloodvein for the rest of the freight. It was still a heavy load for that road, most of it being fir flooring, which would weigh well over a ton. I was looking at it doubtfully, for the mild weather had thawed much of the snow, when Mike Elias, the trader who owned the place where I had stored my freight [see photo, p. 36], came out and told his man Sinnigan to hitch up his team and give me a hand with the freight halfway to Little Grand. From there the road was much better, for there was more snow, and much of it was hard with ice. We camped at the far side of Goose Lake, a little more than halfway to Little Grand, and I hoped to make it from there in a day, a distance of about thirty-six miles, I judged.

We got up early, Sinnigan hoping to get back home that day with the empty sleigh, and I trying to make Little

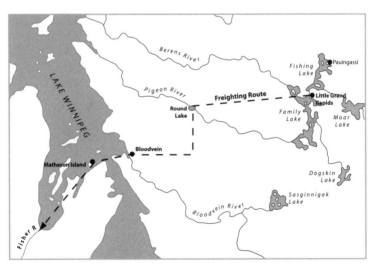

Winter freighting route between Bloodvein and Little Grand Rapids

New Year's Day

Grand. But here I went wrong: being in a hurry, I didn't have my morning devotion of prayer. It was very early, just getting daylight when we said good-bye to each other. I hadn't gone very far down the same trail we had driven a few days before with the three teams—when suddenly the ice broke. First the load went down, then the horses. They were a spirited team and fought terribly to get out, cutting their chests on the ice. The only thing that stayed on top was the load's end.

I unharnessed the horses and tried to pull them out by choking them, to no avail. Then I remembered a native camp of several families on the north side of Goose Lake, about three miles away. I left the horses and ran—no, I couldn't run, for on the way to Bloodvein I had doubled up my sleigh and going up a bare hill, the horses had gone fast, my right foot had caught a stump, and I had broken a bone. So after limping and hobbling along, I arrived at the camp, only to find it deserted.

As I hustled back to my horses, I waved my parka and yelled all I could. The horses were more quiet now but still alive, so I took my ice chisel and tried to make a channel toward shore, which wasn't too far away. Soon I hit thicker ice, and the bottom was not far down, but very soft. I slanted the cut in the ice, chopped some trees and spruce branches, and shoved them down into the mud along with some of my horse blankets.

I got hold of Princess, and just as I was leading her along the channel I had chopped, a native and his son arrived. I begged them to get hold of the rope. They pulled, but as soon as Princess struggled, the teenaged lad ran away, and no coaxing could bring him back. So the father (Andrew Boucher) and I pulled and pulled, and wonder of wonders— Princess came out.

We tried Bob, who was a bit heavier, but it was no go, so I harnessed Princess, and we pulled Bob out. He just lay there and looked like a goner. I rubbed and rubbed him. His eyes seemed glazed over, but finally I got him up, and Andrew and his son helped me unload. I pulled the sleigh out with the team, we loaded up again, and away we went, with more than one prayer of thanks. We did make it to Little Grand that night, though a bit late. Since then, no matter how in a hurry I am, I never start days without first meeting my Lord in prayer.

Daniel's Birth and Delivering Other Babies

On January 21st, 1929, our fifth son, Daniel Roderick, was born. It was quite an ordeal for me. I had arranged for Mrs. Johnnie Moar, a recognized expert midwife, to come over, but very soon she called me in. There was a bit of difficulty in Daniel's arrival, and she was afraid. I had to take over!

The news soon got around, and if ever there was a difficulty in the birth or after birth, I was called. I remember one instance at the Roman Catholic mission site, because this had never before happened in Little Grand. Maingan Boucher had birthed a baby son, but everyone was frightened, for there was still movement. The next day I was asked to come over, and upon examining her I announced there was another baby coming! The second boy arrived shortly. Isaak and Jacob were the first twins in Little Grand Rapids.

New Arrivals

In the meantime, David Nanawin, son of Chief Cubby Nanawin of Poplar River, had arrived as our missionary helper and interpreter. He replaced James Kirkness, who later became the missionary at Pikangikum. We partitioned the front room off with a curtain, and used that as David's quarters. He was a good worker, always had a friendly and winning smile, and was a great help to us.

That winter we had another surprise. We heard that Mr. Street had taken his organ apart and shipped it in three boxes to Little Grand Rapids. When the freight teams delivered the boxes, we found the organ parts inside, covered with snow. After carefully cleaning them, putting them together, and warming the lovely organ up, we looked around and inquired, but not a soul could play. I had had many years of violin lessons, but knew nothing whatsoever about the piano or organ. I could pick out a one-note tune handily, so I cut up some coloured paper and pasted the pieces on the keys that harmonized. Well it wasn't too long before I was playing a hymn every morning in our short religious opening exercises before the school session.

We always started punctually at 9:00, had one short recess at 10:30, and lunch at noon, which I always cooked, at first on our big pot-bellied, cordwood-burning heater. We had individually marked dishes, cups, etc., for each pupil, as a precaution against tuberculosis, which was rampant in Little Grand Rapids and which we attacked with vigour.

So thanks to the goodness of Mr. Street, we now had an organ for our school, which still held the Sunday service. We wanted to improve the building with desks, flooring, and roof shingles. However, the Indian Department informed me that they could not pay the whole shot, as the freight was too prohibitive. I told them that if they would give us the material, I could freight it up free of charge. This they did, and we now had a halfway decent school building.

A Trip to Bloodvein

I believe it was April 19th when I started off on a trip to Bloodvein River with my friend Dave Donaldson, a Hudson's Bay clerk, and Jack Cotton, a trader. Mail and provisions were among the reasons. We took Bob and Princess and, I believe, Dobbin, but got only as far as Goose Lake, about twenty-five miles from Little Grand, when we noticed the lake was open in the centre and ducks were swimming around. After a lengthy debate, Dave and I started out to see if we could make Bloodvein on foot, leaving Mr. Cotton with the horses, which had ample pasture. We intended to travel light, so all we took was a canvas (piece of duck), one frying pan, two spoons, and a little bag of oatmeal. Oh, to be young and foolish again!

We made it across the lake a bit farther east, then got back to the trail, much of it under water with a little crust of ice on top. Dave, quite an athletic chap and proud of it, was always a step or two ahead of me until noon, when we stopped for lunch. Our meal was one frying pan of porridge. I drew a line through the middle, we each ate half, then were off again.

Pretty soon Dave started to lag a bit, and around four o'clock he looked ahead at a long stretch of open muskeg and said, "Let's go back."

It took me a little time to persuade him to continue. Finally I pointed to a bluff of poplars in the far distance and said, "Look, Dave, I think that's Spring Camp, where there's a stove and a bunk." I was right, and we dead tired fellows were glad, having come nearly forty miles under very adverse conditions.

I cooked another frying pan of porridge, a little fuller this time, and we went to it. I finished my half, but Dave couldn't quite make his. "And you a Scotsman straight from Aberdeen," I teased while finishing the balance. Soon we rolled into the hay-filled bunk and covered ourselves with the piece of canvas. Dave tried all night to get a bigger share of it, but found me too heavy to move.

Next day we arrived in Bloodvein in good shape and in good time. All that we had expected was there, but what were we going to do about it? Mike Elias, God rest his soul, told his man Sinnigan to re-shoe his team of horses and give them to us. It was overwhelming to find such generosity. I don't know if I would have loaned my team under such conditions. I told him that if I lost them through the ice I would replace them, that I'd look after them all summer, and bring them back over the road the first thing in the fall.

We were never to see Mike again. He broke through the ice and drowned, out in the bay. They found some matches and cigarette paper, and a mitt, suggesting that he had lit a cigarette and started to cough, as he often did, and broke through. They recovered his body right there.

Dave and I made it back in good time. It started to snow, and we ran across a big flock of Canada Geese. Dave tried to get one, for they couldn't fly, being all wet with snow, but he didn't quite make it. When we came to Goose Lake, we went back to where we had crossed going down and tested the ice with our chisel. Almost halfway across, a native named Andrew Boucher came to meet us, and gave us an awful dressing-down for doing such a foolish and risky thing. Being reunited with our horses and Jack Cotton, we made it home easily the next day, April 26th, which I believe is a record for arriving in Little Grand with horses.

Developing the Mission

THE SUMMER OF 1929 WAS A VERY BUSY ONE. There was so much to do in every day that often we wished we were twins. Good headway was being made in clearing our grounds of trees and stumps, and after the leaves and brush were raked, we found a lot of rock boulders of great size. Working till dark when we were free, with pry bars we managed to roll the boulders down the bank to the rocky side of the lake. By now we had a fairly large garden and managed to plow it for the first time; then there was fencing to do. We got the very best page wire because our goats were agile and nimble of feet. But we found out, to our delight, that they were great brush clearers. The back of our home began to take on the appearance of a park—everything cleared away for six or more feet, and the trees clearly defined in their natural beauty, since we had also fenced off the house and put in flowers.

Ernest, Herman, Albert, and Rolf with garden produce

6

CLOSE TO THE GALLOWS
1929 to 1930

Forest Fires

Talk about evacuation—the natives were masters at it. When fear gripped them, the tents were down and the people gone with their belongings in a few minutes! I witnessed this many times. One big forest fire that threatened the whole community and reserve at Little Grand Rapids was probably caused by lightning, for the native people were always very careful with their fires, dousing them with much water when they were through. This fire came from the north, driven by a strong northwest wind on an almost two-mile front. In no time at all, the entire reserve was evacuated, and there were many houses by that time. As it drew toward evening, the fire began to look fiercer and fiercer.[7]

Our old friend James Kirkness had been a missionary helper at Oxford House, I believe, and had helped me in the building of our church and in holding services. He always carried his big Cree Bible with him, and was now a missionary in Pikangikum. He had come down during the summer holidays with his family, and was camping in a tent on our mission grounds. Even he decided to move, and I didn't blame him, for great big pieces of burning birch bark were falling all around us, and the thick brushy woods were only a few yards from our house.

Gusti was worried, and asked me what we ought to do. I said, "Take the children and put them to bed."

I had taken the boys out in the canoe and let them have a good look at the fire, which was clearly visible for miles. Then I came up and stood a while watching, all the time hoping and praying that we would be spared. After Gusti had gone, I went down to the shore, pushed my canoe out, and watched. It was a fierce, wild, awesome sight, the wind blowing steadily in our direction, the fire now only about half a mile away. It had jumped the lake onto the reserve at a point a mile across from us. Luckily, some people saw it and managed to put it out.

A great calm had come over me in the canoe. "Lord," I said, "this is all Thine. Thou canst save it if Thou wilt!" And

Gusti, Fritz and the goats

do you know, I had hardly stopped speaking when the wind stopped, then actually turned in the opposite direction. It was a great moment of quiet faith given at a time of need. We were saved.

After that I went to work on that brush near our house, mostly scrub spruce with a few bigger trees of poplar and birch. I pretty well cleared it right away, with only a few stumps left. Well, during one of my trips soon after, Richard dug out the stumps and turned the whole thing over. We fenced it, and it became one of our most productive potato patches. Richard did this all on his own volition, and it was a heartwarming experience to see the co-operative spirit developing in our family, as it more often does in rural districts than in urban ones.

Around this time we contacted our brother Rodi, who was now living in Berens River with his wife, Gusti's sister. The whole trading post at Poplar River—the store, warehouse, and house—had been wiped out by a tremendous forest fire.[8] They had lost everything while away on a business trip. My Dad nearly lost his life, as there was quite a wind, and he could not get the canoe off the sand into the water. He had to lie in the water while the fire wiped everything out, including the bedding and cash he had brought down from the store. There, in the water, the natives found him. Nothing had been insured, so the bridges were completely burned, removing every temptation to ever want to turn back again.

Spousal Abuse

In the meantime, there was further trouble at Little Grand Rapids. Some of the men were pounding their wives unmercifully. One day the chief came to me and said one of the wives refused to go out with her husband on the trapline, because she was certain he would kill her, as his beatings were getting worse every winter. You see, it was the wives' duty to go out from camp into the deep snow and cut wood, then pack it out on their backs. They wore skirts, never pants, and sometimes had to go quite a distance, as the dry wood had been pretty much thinned out through the years. When I heard this I was boiling mad, for the men mostly lay beside the warm fire and smoked after they came home from their trapline or hunt. Now the chief was also stirred up, because he thought a good deal of the woman who refused to go out again. I told him to call a meeting of all the men.

The school was full and I landed into them, closing with the words: "If some of you want to fight so much, why don't you pick on someone who can fight back. You are just rank cowards."

One particular man I had raked over the coals jumped up and came toward the front, mad as a wet hen. I was mad too, the Lord forgive me, and I jumped down from the platform to meet him. I would have hit him, I know, if he had come any closer. However, he backed down and went back to his seat. Believe it or not, this ended the wife pounding, but it had a strange result. For soon afterward I heard that the women were pounding their men, and wilfully destroying some of the men's properties.

One night, in the wee small hours, there was a knock at our door. It was the reserve constable. He was quite excited.

He said, "Come quickly, John Keeper is dying. His wife hit him over the head with a two-by-four."

I took my kit, stethoscope and all, and hastened to the place. The husband was lying in the front room on the floor, his wife wailing loudly in the bedroom. I took his pulse, stethoscoped his heart, felt his head. There was nothing at all the matter with the man. He was shamming, but I didn't give him away. I went to the woman and told her that her husband would be all right, but that she'd better be careful, she had come pretty close to the gallows and being hanged.

However, this was not the end of it. I was down near the barn when I saw one of our younger, heavier men come down the hill with several other young men following him. At once I sensed there was something wrong. This young man had come out on top in all the tests of strength, etc., in a recent celebration.

As he came up, he was loudly proclaiming, "What kind of law have you brought to us?" And then, "What cheer?" Stretching forth his hand, he grabbed mine. I was ready for him, and before he knew it, he was on his back, and a good boy thereafter. So the testing went on in various ways, and the work multiplied.

Feeding the Hungry

Gusti, seeing the people hungry all the time, said one day, "I would like to see them filled up!"

"Let's do it," I said.

We had our warehouse full. Mrs. Joe Alix, a trader's wife, helped cook and bake. When the day came, the canoes arrived from every direction. What tables we had were used by the elderly; the rest sat under the birch trees. It was a fine summer day. I prayed that the Lord would bless this occasion. They all came—pagans, Roman Catholics, our people—and they ate and ate till they could eat no more. The widows took their big bandana handkerchiefs off, knotted them, and filled them with all they would hold, and still there was more. The Lord really blessed everyone that day, which we will never, never forget.

Fritz, the Dog

Our family was well, our house comfortable and warm, and our warehouse full of supplies for the whole year. We had a registered Alsatian by the name of Fritz, who became a full member of the family, and of whom I will tell from time to time, about things he did that somehow pointed to a super-intelligence. When I first brought him home with two other Alsatians (one coal black, the other a female), Gusti was horrified. She had heard of the viciousness of this type of dog. But I assured her: "It depends how they are brought up. Let us discourage all aggressiveness."

The other two we sold and gave away, one to the game warden, the other to our brother. Fritz became a great companion to our boys, but one evening Gusti came in quite disgusted. She said, "That is a fine dog you brought us; he lets the neighbours' dogs eat all his food."

"Well," I said, "we have discouraged all aggressiveness. You just take a stick next time, and let him know that these dogs do not belong here."

That was all that was necessary, for Fritz grew into a fine big dog, weighing a hundred pounds before he was a year old. He became a great protector of our goats. No more dogs were allowed on the place, and woe to any dog that resisted him. We had to discourage him from killing other dogs, mostly sleigh dogs belonging to the natives. One day Fritz found a very stubborn dog who would not go, so he rolled him into the lake, and the last we saw, he was swimming in chase after the dog, over half a mile away.

When the little goats came, he used to lick them dry before he let the mother go near them. One mistake he made, though. One night he tackled a skunk. He did not like himself for quite a while after that.

Speaking of skunks, while Fritz was still small and in the house, I became aware that skunks were working around the house. So I made a deadfall with a figure-four-construction.[9] We were hardly in bed when I heard a thump. I ran out in my nightshirt and found a dead skunk as flat as a pancake under the heavy stone-weighted top. I set it again, but didn't do a very good job in the dark, for when I heard another thump and ran out, a skunk was pulling away from the deadfall. I took a washing line prop and killed him.

Supplies for the Destitute

More troubles lay ahead. When we took over administering the destitute supplies, the chief and his councillors came, expecting to get their rations of flour, bacon, and tea. I gave them a good talking-to, explaining that the rations were only for the sick, the helpless, and the old widows, and that they were men and should prove their manhood by not accepting anything they had not earned. This did not go over very well. However, they got used to it, and I believe felt the better for it, for there was always a certain jealousy attached—one always thinking that the other got more.

I tried to get rid of handling the destitute supplies, but the Indian Agent, Mr. Andrew Irwin, said, "No, Luther, there is no one else. Accept this as your cross that you must bear."

It was the same with the bales of clothing we received from the kind United Church women.

Not only jealousy, but greed and selfishness reared their ugly heads amongst the natives, and I found our whole system in dealing with our Indian people absolutely wrong. Instead of making them self-supporting, we made them more and more dependent on charity.

At Little Grand we showed them how to make gardens and grow things, and I can still remember one man coming over, holding some beautiful cucumbers, which he had grown and wondered at. There was no need to be hungry, with fish in the lake and good soil to grow things, but the people were hungry. Prices of groceries were high: flour, $25 a sack; butter, $3 a pound; sugar, 50 cents a pound, and so on.

The five dollars per head the natives received each treaty time was all gone within a few minutes, most always foolishly spent. So at one treaty time, I asked the Indian Agent, "Why not give these people food instead of money—flour, tea, rice, sugar, bacon, and so on?" He said, "I'll see what I can do."

I thought no more of it, figuring it had come to naught, but to my surprise, I got a radio message one day: "Meet me at Berens River with fifteen canoes." The traders laughed, wondering where I'd get fifteen canoes.

I had three myself, and got ten more. So down we went to Berens River, and what a difference—prices were so low! Flour was only $2.10 a hundred, etc. We made two trips and freighted it all up. The local stores naturally suffered a great

Luther and bear cub; Herman, Ernest, and Rolf. Richard standing by sunflower. House with kitchen-dispensary at rear

loss at the time, but I had talked to them before, hoping for reduced prices, and was told it was impossible. The prices came way down after that, and for a while living conditions were better, as far as food was concerned.

The Dispensary

Spring finally came, and with it, more and more work. We extended the house by building a 26-by-14 ft. addition for a kitchen and dispensary, since we had quite an enlarged dispensary now. We also placed some seating there, for the room was often filled with people who wanted medicines and tooth extractions. I became known as the most practical dentist in a wide region. The Indian Department doctor who visited yearly never had to pull another tooth. Gusti was my assistant. I had no Novocain at first. Most of the natives were more afraid of the needle than of the tooth-pulling.

Whenever I went to Winnipeg, I took lessons from Dr. Roy Bier, one of the foremost exodontists in Canada, a fine Christian man who helped me a lot in many ways. I know

School children in outdoor class

one time he heard me out when I came to him quite discouraged about the spiritual progress in our community. I was sitting in the dentist chair (he had pulled nine of my teeth), so he was very close as he turned his big brown eyes upon me and said, "I wonder what Christ thinks of our progress?"

I said no more, but went back with a greater sense of enthusiasm than ever before. Dr. Bier gave me many instruments—besides forceps, things for root extractions, Novocain, syringes, and needles. He also gave me some ointment he had invented, which was already being used by missionaries as far away as China without having been approved by the medical profession. He called it Healatone, and I believe he had it made by Parker-Davis. We will tell you more of this later on.

My dear Gusti thoroughly disliked holding the patient's head, and claims to this day that this was the beginning of her stomach pains (which later developed into ulcers when four of our boys were in the armed services). Be that as it may, she was a great helpmate, for I pulled hundreds of teeth during the eleven years in Little Grand Rapids, including some of Gusti's and our children's.

I well remember one night. There was a loud scream from upstairs where the boys slept. Gusti was up there in a moment, and when she came down, she said Ernie had a terrible toothache. "We'll soon fix that!" I said, selecting my forceps. The tooth was out in no time, and Ernie was sleeping peacefully in a matter of minutes.

That summer, too, I made a new experiment. As the people were all living on our side and on the island in front of the Hudson's Bay post, I saw no need for taking them across to the school. I brought all the desks over, and held school outside on our grounds. It seldom rained in the spring months; however, I set up our big tent as a precaution. It was a great success, and I did gain a lot by it, for Gusti could cook the meals for the noon lunch. We had a very good attendance.[10]

I must mention another thing about the kitchen. I had two big windows installed on the south side, and Gusti always had a beautiful panorama of the lake, the lovely evergreen-covered islets, and the far shore. She, being a woman, could never see any use in sparing water, so we always had to be on the alert, or else she'd be carrying the heavy three-gallon pails from the lake up the hill to the house, a distance of over a hundred yards.

So I got a big galvanized tank that easily held forty gallons, and gave the boys the duty to see that it was always full, and they did. I can still see them, Herman in the lead with the big pails, then Ernie with the smaller ones, down to the youngest who wanted to carry water, too. So Mom had to put handles on some jam tins, and we never had to admonish them. If one forgot coming home from school, the other soon reminded him that they had to fill the tank. From that day on Mom never had to worry about water.

I also had a new kitchen stove freighted up, and our first gasoline-powered washing machine. As the summers were very warm and we always had quite a bit of milk, we needed a cooler of some kind. So we built an ice-house with a heavily insulated double door and double walls—

one log house built inside another, with about a foot of space between the walls, which we filled with moss. We stocked the inside with ice from the lake, and always had ice over the next summer.

Gideon's Birth

As June drew to a close [1930], on the 28th to be exact, we were expecting another little stranger, as the natives used to say. So I hustled over to Mrs. Moar. She came, kind soul, but again was full of fear. Anyway, I said I would be close by. This was very awkward, as school was over and the children were all at home, it being midday. I gathered them around and told them to stay at the beach and keep a sharp lookout, for I had heard that the stork would bring us another baby—and we don't want another one, do we?

Herman, Ernest, and Albert carrying water up from the lake

They were all in accord: No, we don't want another baby. So I said, "You watch, he will come over the lake and you should be able to see him from afar, and when you see him let me know, and I will shoot him."

I never thought about the difficulty of shooting a stork carrying a baby, but no one brought it up, so there they stayed, and sure enough, pretty soon I got the signal that I was wanted. Everything went well, and we had our sixth boy, Gideon Sigmund. We named him Sigmund after Gusti's brother, who was also born on June 28th, as it was with Daniel and my brother Roderick, who were both born on January 21st.

Now we had our six boys, and that is what we wanted. Before I proposed to my wife I had told her I liked large families, and that I would like to have six boys and she could have six girls. It didn't stop her from marrying me!

7

EIGHT GOTHIC WINDOWS

1930 to 1931

Rodi and Dad Come Up

Brother Rodi was always efficient in tackling mechanical problems, so he came to Little Grand and went to work to finish our house. It was no mean job. The logs weren't evenly hewed, so he cut boards into three-inch strips and sided the whole big room to perfectly level walls and ceiling. He also divided it into two bedrooms, a front room, and a dining room. The kitchen was built onto the west side. The rooms then were sheeted with the ten-test. [Ten-test was a cheap, fibrous wood that came in sheets used as a base under siding.] It was a wonderful home. With only a small wood-burning heater, it kept us warm in the fiercest storms and coldest weather when the temperature plunged to 50° or 60° below. We never had to get up at night to put more wood on. We even grew an orange tree of good size.

Later on that fall, we were all glad when Dad came up to live with us again. He had been with us from 1922 to 1927, and we missed him. We gave him a bedroom all his own. He was a great help, for no matter how much I remonstrated with him, he insisted that he saw the wood for the stoves. I always had plenty of wood piled up, hauled out with the horses—tamarack for the heater, and jackpine mostly for the cook stove. Grandpa became very fond of Rolf, who never was too well or too strong.

Weddings, Medicines, Vital Statistics

Now, thanks to Rodi, we were quite comfortable in a house where we would live longer than in any previous house, almost eleven years. I believe we would still be there if the Church hadn't transferred us to Berens River in 1938. We were comfortable and reasonably happy, but never had much time, for I had received more work. Besides being acting Indian Agent, which entailed the handling of destitute supplies, we received our provincial certificate to perform marriages. Most of the people had not been married legally. I remember one family of seven or eight whom I baptized all

Luther chatting with the Deer Lakers after a church service

at once and then married the parents. Then I became dispenser of medicines for the whole district as well as registrar of vital statistics.[11]

It was a busy year in 1930, and I often think it is a good thing we cannot see ahead and must learn to live just for the day, leaving the future in God's hands, knowing that all things work together for good, to them that love God (Romans 8:28). This we still had to learn, and it was a very bitter lesson.

Building a Church[12]

Beginning to feel really at home, we now made plans to build a church. Ordinarily, the right process would have been to ask the Presbytery's permission, and through the due course of procedure, would have thus begun. But we were out of touch with the rest of the Church, and the usual meetings for our Presbytery were held in Norway House, a few hundred miles away. As a matter of fact, we never left the place for about five years, other than to freight in supplies. We felt we couldn't leave our people who were helpless against the white man's guile. Furthermore, we felt the matter of the church was between the Lord and us, that we were abundantly blessed to do this ourselves. However, later on we did apply to the Home Mission Board and did get some aid.[13]

To put up any kind of a building in Little Grand Rapids was expensive because of the freight rate, and even the logs were few and far between, that is, any good-sized ones, for we wanted to build a fair-sized church. So we scouted around and found that we had to go as far as fourteen miles in scattered places. We wanted the logs hewn on both sides. We let the contract to a few responsible men who were not freighting up the river, as the summer months usually were busy with freighting up supplies by canoe for the Hudson's Bay Company and the trading posts. It was really the only means of livelihood during the summer. The rate at the time was about eight dollars per hundred, mostly taken out in trade. It was a joy to see these nimble men (mostly only weighing about 150 pounds) with their small feet, many only size four, going over steep portages with 300 and 400 hundred pounds on their pack-strap. They were brought up to it and used to it.

Our plans were made and our needs for lumber and material figured out, not only for the church, but also for the inside finishing of the house. It was quite an undertaking—too much to handle, I felt, for our hackney team of Bob and Princess. So we wrote to Mr. James McKinnon Coutts, the secretary of Campbell Bros. and Wilson and also the Wholesalers Trust Company, to ship these orders and a heavier team out to Matheson Island and to Bloodvein River, late in the fall. This they did, as my credit was good, having been in the store business for several years. I always found James McKinnon Coutts to be a very gracious, dependable, and kindly man.

Oh, to be young again, and to have the courage to go out into the unknown without a qualm or a doubt, but knowing that the good Lord will bless and see it through even seemingly impossible difficulties.

That summer I was busy hauling logs with my old trusted two-horse Evinrude. The natives snagged the logs down to the lakeshore where I nailed them together, two by two, and tied one pair behind the other, usually taking six logs. They were quite large and long for that country. Then unloading at our shore, the grey team pulled them up the hill above the mission house where we intended to build the church. It took a while to get them all up. After we had them laid out in their proper place, we each took a corner and dovetailed them. Then we countersunk all the stringers for the floor. It was quite an undertaking. I forget the length and breadth, but believe it was 32 by 40 feet.

Once all the walls were up, the roof was soon on. I did practically all the shingling myself, not only the top, but the gable ends also. But a great problem remained. We hadn't put in any windows, for I wanted them with Gothic tops.

Our men had never seen such, so we had only cut in the door. I didn't know what I'd let myself in for! When I finally received the eight Gothic windows, and proceeded to chop out the logs, I found they were bone dry and not easily cut. Late that fall we finally got all of them in.

Next we engaged some of the natives to cut a wide swath of trees for an opening toward the lake. This became our cemetery, and little did we dream at the time that it would hold some of the ones most dear to us.

Trouble with the Trader

Now winter came, and we had to get ready to freight up all the supplies for the inside of the house. Ten-test was the biggest item, and good fir flooring and lumber for stripping, then the lumber and shingles for the church, and sacks of oats. The team that came out was a dandy—grey Percherons of 16 to 18 hundredweight. They could really pull a load. David Nanawin drove them all winter and even made some trips alone when I couldn't get away.

In the meantime, the Hudson's Bay asked me if my teams could bring in some supplies for them. I thought it was a good thing, for the income of that freight would help me pay my expenses. Here is where the trouble started. One of the free traders resented this. He had teams of his own but not often very good teamsters, and it was a difficult road. Often they had to leave freight along the way, and once a horse died on the trip. So it was reported to the Inspector of Indian Agencies in Winnipeg that I was neglecting my duties as a teacher. I was surprised, for we were teaching three of this man's children, and they shared in everything, even though this was an Indian Department School. The fact was, once in a while I had David Nanawin take over the teaching when I had to be elsewhere. For me to give such assistance was really the main purpose of the Church, and David was a certified first class Manitoba teacher, fully capable to teach the low grades. The accusation that I had left an unqualified teacher in charge was soon cleared up, but it left a bitter taste in my mouth—until I remembered our Lord, and then I really felt elated.

Haying

Two teams needed a lot of hay, at least twelve tons, and the goats needed about six tons. So it was necessary to make nearly twenty tons of hay, which was no mean feat using a scythe in places that had never been cut before. I remember one place where we found lots of hay. It was "kmeenominat-ickcookat" meaning "rice-making place." It [Rice Lake] was about fifteen miles south on our Family Lake. Poor Richard—home for the summer, he was initiated here. The flies bothered him terribly, so someone suggested he should take some syrup out of our grub box and put it on his hair. The flies then really singled him out as their prime target.

At lunchtime we were situated at a windy, rocky point. Seeing a lot of leeches, we fished some out and put them on the rock. Invariably these creatures would make for the water, so someone suggested we'd have ourselves a race. There were five of us, so we lined them all up and let them go. It was really a horse race in miniature, though quite slow. Some would start out well then fall by the wayside, while others that started out behind often came in first. It was really quite a diversion, and a great help in facing the flies.

Many amusing incidents happened, one or two at the Old Fort. A mile or so up the creek from the main lake, there was a little lake. One day while cutting there it was very hot, no wind, not a cloud in the sky, and all the granite rock around us giving off reflected sun, which seemed in double force. Our drinking water was soon diminished. Most of us just bit our lips and endured it, but not Richard and one other. They laid down their handkerchiefs in the soupy yellow water amongst the reeds and frogs and tadpoles, and sucked up this awful warm liquid.

A few days afterwards when we were stacking this hay, we stopped for lunch at the noon hour and observed

Richard taking a little frog out from his pants. The creature had climbed up inside, and when Richard quickly put him down, he insisted on coming back. Everyone laughed, and someone suggested that Richard hatched this frog because he had drunk the yellow water, and that the little frog was coming back to him because he took Richard for his mamma. Poor Richard, the laugh was on him!

However, that fall the laugh was on me. You see, we had to get the hay home by water in good time, so I built a hayrack out of poles, tied it on my two 19-foot canoes, and used my 17-foot canoe and two-horsepower Evinrude as a tug. The native people said it was quite an eerie sight to see a big load of hay (over a ton) coming along over the water, because at first they couldn't see the little canoe towing it. This time we were getting the last of the hay at the Old Fort. Joe Potvin (our "Frenchman") and I had been bringing in the loads and pitching them up to Richard, who was building the haystack on the hayrack. When we pulled down the creek to the last bunch, I sized up the stack, saw we couldn't get it all on, and told Richard to come down and help Joe while I went up and tried to widen the load by tramping it down. I must have stepped a little too far on the outside corner, and down I went headfirst into the creek. When I came up, weeds clinging over my head, I must have looked like old Neptune himself. I expected Richard and Joe to be standing there roaring with laughter, but they were solemn as two old owls. Later I asked them why they didn't laugh. "Well," one of them said, "we sure felt like it, you looked so funny, but we were afraid to!"

David Nanawin Leaves Little Grand Rapids

David Nanawin was leaving us, going back home to Poplar River. We missed him, for he was always a willing worker with a smile on his face. I remember one time he made a late trip in the spring. The snow had been unusually deep, and the road cut up badly by other freight sleighs. I was worried, expecting him the same day, and took off across the lake. Coming over the portage to the shore of another small lake, I spotted David with his sleigh deep down in the snow. He jumped off, shovelled, then started the horses, which were always willing and steady pullers. He walked alongside the sleigh, resting the team now and then, until he got across the lake and saw me. I have never forgotten that witness of a good and faithful young man.

David still writes to us. He enlisted during the last war, and became blind while stationed at the Aleutian Islands.

Roderick McDonald, the Third Interpreter

Roderick McDonald was coming up [from Berens River] with his native wife and two daughters to help in the missionary work. We built them a house, a little to the southeast of ours. Roderick, part native, was a big man with curly reddish hair and a slight limp caused by an old hip injury. There was lots of fun in Roderick. He was always telling jokes, most of them on the Scots.

I am not good at remembering jokes, but one of his has somehow stayed with me. It goes like this: There was an accident at a sawmill. One of the men, who was of Scottish descent, had his finger cut off by the saw. They gave him first aid, bandaged the wound, and then someone said, "Hey, where is that finger? If we get Mac to the doc he might be able to save it for him."

So they dug around in the sawdust but couldn't find a thing. Then another Scot came up and asked, "What's the matter?"

"Well, we cannot find Mac's finger. The doc might save it for him."

"Ooch! But that's easy." He opened his purse and threw a dime on the sawdust—and lo and behold, the finger came wiggling right out after it.

Anyway, whenever I could not find Gusti, I would look down to the garden or the barn, and there Roderick would be, leaning on something, telling her a joke.

Roderick also made a good interpreter, for he was fearless

and told the offenders exactly what I said. One time, though, when I had given a councillor a dressing down, he told me, "Gee, I felt sorry for that man of what you told him, but you were right." And here is something for a psychiatrist to figure out—this councillor became the best friend I had! In the last stages of winter when fish were scarce, he would bring me the first big fish he caught. He found out that I liked the brains of animals, and whenever he shot a moose or deer he brought over the brains and the choicest piece of meat.

Translating Languages

The year 1931 really shook us before it was over, and almost made us lose our faith. It began very promisingly in every way. We were getting to be more fluent in the Anishinabe language and could carry on in many ways without an interpreter. However, translating Bible quotations was another matter. I have seen men stumped when interpreting some sermons; they had spoken that language all their lives, but never had much contact with spiritual matters.

I also found out that the hymn books, the Bible, and the New Testaments that we were given for use by our church people were not written in the Anishinabe language, but in Cree. This really astonished me, for the two languages are vastly different. It's almost like giving an English-speaking congregation a Bible and hymn book in French. For instance, the word for dog in Cree is Atim, whereas for the Anishinabe it is Anemush. However, some biblical words seemed the same, and the syllabics were easily mastered by the natives. Words like soul, life, God, and Jesus, were the same, so I imagine the people got something out of it. I intended, when I had the time, to see what could be done about translating our hymn books and Bible into the Anishinabe language. However, our interpreter knew both languages, and we managed to straighten out quite a few things.

Dobbin the Buckskin Mare

Our good neighbour friend, Rev. John Niddrie, wanted the grey team. We didn't have to freight that much up anymore, so Bob and Princess were enough for us. We sent the team down to him, and he was quite pleased with them.

Johnnie Moar wanted to sell me his buckskin pony called Dobbin, which he had sent up from Berens River. Dobbin was quite a mare. I saw Johnnie walking alongside the toboggan with only a few bags of flour on it. I told him he should ride, for that was no load for Dobbin. He said he'd tried, but as soon as he sat on her, she wouldn't go. This was on the Bloodvein road, so Dobbin and I had a good "talk," and after I was through with her she pulled almost anything. She was a tough little mare, easily kept, so we bought her. She became quite a standby in our family.

We lost Dobbin's colt one day when we swam the horses across the river below the falls. It was a bit rough, the wind against the current making short waves. She must have got water into her lungs, for she just tipped over on her side, dead.

Outboard Motors

The summer of 1931 went by in the usual manner, except for one thing. I had to make a painful decision. We had been using outboard motors for some time. As a matter of fact, my brother and I were the first ones to use an outboard motor up the Berens River to Little Grand Rapids, freighting. We were told it could not be done, that the river was too treacherous and too rocky. The first trip was quite a trial, all right. Our guide, who was born and raised there and had made many trips up the river, often steered us right on top of a rock. We broke many shear-off pins and had to hammer out the bronze propeller time and again. But soon we proved it was the only way to freight up that river, for portaging and paddling or rowing against that strong current was a killing job, and made it a long trip.

So now every native who could swing it would own an outboard motor. But not knowing too much about motors, they were always in trouble. And where would they go for help, but to the man who knew all about them. I was glad to be of service, but there were natives from Deer Lake coming through from Pikangikum, Poplar Hill, and everywhere, and the first thing I knew, I was doing nothing but repair work! Finally I had to tell them I was not sent up here just to work on outboard motors, and they would have to learn to do it themselves. Even then I could not refuse them completely.

Our house with the dormer Rodi built

Church with gothic windows; warehouse on right

8

DEMONS, DEATH, AND THE
NEWLY AWAKENED
1931 to 1932

Treaty Time

I believe it was in the summer of 1931 that Mr. Niddrie asked me to take him around on a treaty trip. Mr. Niddrie started preaching in Scotland at age nineteen, then went out as a missionary in the north, and later at Berens River. He loved the native people deeply and they sensed it, and loved him in return. The trip was quite an undertaking, for we couldn't use a big canoe on account of the long portages. We took Sasho Keeper along as our bowsman, and Mr. Street, the teacher from Berens River, came also. We figured Mr. Niddrie weighed close to five hundred pounds, and when he got into the canoe it really showed. However, he was a perfect canoe man and kept good balance, which is not often the case with some white men. I've had an RCMP constable in my canoe who almost upset us several times, until I asked him to leave his leggings and spurs off.

On these treaty trips you were certain to find the natives at home. It was always quite an occasion. The old muzzle-loaders boomed out a salute of welcome. The flags flew, and all the women wore their best. A doctor, a Mounted Policeman, and a clerk would also be along. Crisp new dollar bills were handed out to every man, woman, and child, with the chief and councillors receiving a bit extra.

We travelled with Mr. Niddrie around the same time, though not with the party, and stopped at Poplar Hill where payments were made. There we held a service with some baptisms and weddings, then went on to Pikangikum where other payments were to be made. Pikangikum is quite a way into Ontario. The scenery at this time of year was lovely, evergreens setting a darker background of green to the lighter-coloured poplars and birches and willows. Yellow to golden water lilies were everywhere to be seen. Where the water on the lakes was still, the loveliest snow-white lilies floated like stars.

On this trip, the treaty party left a day ahead of us because there was so much for us to do in Pikangikum. When we left the next day, Sasho Keeper said he had once

Forestry's Vickers Vedette flies over Waco on the U.C. Mission beach

travelled a shortcut from a point close to Poplar Hill to Deer Lake, where we would next meet the treaty party. So I said, "Let's take it!"

But was I sorry afterward. We went up a creek that came to an end, so we had to unload and proceed on foot. Sasho went on ahead with a load, while I followed with the canoe to which I had bolted a yoke in the centre. I didn't get very far before I was crawling on my hands and knees under fallen trees. I managed to keep Sasho in sight, and finally we got across to a little lake.

On the way back I met Mr. Street coming up with a load, and then Mr. Niddrie, who found it very hard going. He censured me for keeping the men working too hard and too late. This was nothing new to me, for I heard it all the time from others when on the road. Sasho and I took the balance of our stuff across and made camp. While Sasho was cooking supper I walked over to a dry tamarack tree and carved my name on it. It was not a very big tree, so I left the "c" and "e" out of Schuetze, and what do you know, when you look at an Esso road map of Manitoba-Ontario, you will find that lake marked Shutze Lake.

Deer Lake

I must say a few words about the Namaepinishik, a band of natives at Deer Lake who impressed me very much. When they embraced Christianity, several had two or three wives. Dr. Barner, who made several trips up there, told them that they could have only one wife when they became Christians. One of the Meakin men [or possibly Meekis] had three wives and wouldn't do it. Dr. Barner told him, "That is not very good."

He replied, "It is very good. They never quarrel with me, only with each other, and all want to please me. One stays home and keeps the house warm and cooks the meals and does the washing. Another one sets snares to catch rabbits, makes rabbit robes, cuts all the firewood, and brings it out to the house. The other one runs in front of my dogsled in the winter, and paddles for me in the bow of my canoe. No! Three is just right." And so he turned Christianity down.

Adam Fiddler became a stout Christian and a leader amongst his people. He had two wives, one quite elderly and one still a teenager. Everyone thought he'd put the old lady away, but he fooled them all. He went over to the Hudson's Bay Company and told them to give his young wife, whom he had married according to Indian custom, all she needed until she married again. Then he built her a brand new house and knew her no more. His brother, Robert Fiddler, became chief, and these two brothers held the Deer Lakers in the palms of their hands. There was no more illegitimacy, no more bad debts, and under Adam's direction they built a church and got three organs, one large and two portables.

There is another story attached to the larger organ. They had ordered it through us at an earlier treaty party, having seen only pictures. They came down to Berens River to freight up the Hudson Bay Company's yearly supplies as well as to get the new organ. The Skootay Shiman (Fire Boat) arrived, and there it was. Well, they sat down and laughed and laughed, and no one could get a word out of them, except to hear someone say, "And we were going to put this in our little canoe!"

The next day when we came to the dock to meet them again, the organ was all in pieces. With screwdrivers and other tools, they had taken it apart. We thought this was the end of it, but we were to get a surprise. Arriving in Deer Lake a few hours ahead of the treaty party, we went into the church for the service—and there in back of the pulpit was the organ!

Near the front on either side were the two small folding organs. As soon as we entered, three young men came forward and asked what hymns we were going to sing. They had the Cree hymn books in syllabics, so Mr. Niddrie told them. Then they asked what tunes we were using. Mr. Niddrie softly whistled the tunes. With grunts of satisfaction, they took their places at the organs. The service began, and all three organs in perfect harmony began the doxology. The whole congregation stood. The church was packed and the singing almost lifted off the roof, very nearly drowning out the organs.

It was an auspicious opening of a service we never forgot. And when it was over, the congregation came forward and placed an offering of 90-odd dollars on the table. Rev. John Niddrie never took up an offering from the natives, perhaps because he intimately knew their desperate poverty, but here at treaty time they had received money, and they wanted to give.

After the treaty we took Mr. Niddrie and Mr. Street safely home to Berens River, a distance of some two hundred miles with many portages. Then it was back up the river again with freight, often bales of clothing from Church missionary societies in Ontario.

Conversion at Little Grand Rapids

We found our natives much more receptive spiritually to the Christian Gospel than our white brethren. It was strange how you could tell the difference: the pagans' eyes seemed black and dead, while those of the newly awakened shone with light. Certainly they were subjected to the white man's temptations and erred and went astray, but there was a decided difference.

When we first arrived, the people were dirty. I never saw anything like it. When I put my stethoscope to the chest of a nice-looking young girl of sixteen, I couldn't see her skin for the crust of dirt. No one ever went into the lovely lake for a swim, since nobody could swim! By the time we left, most of the young people had learned. Once when a nurse came out to bring back a little baby we had taken in for surgery, she remarked, "My, Mr. Schuetze, how white all the washing looks on the line! Much whiter and cleaner than many wash lines near Winnipeg."

We sometimes made trips to Pauingassi just ten miles east of Little Grand Rapids. These people were untouched by the Gospel, bringing to mind the old saying, "Cleanliness is next to godliness."

Gradually our people were emerging from the yoke of superstition and fear. One day the chief told me of an instance that happened on Upon Gashing Lake [now called Fishing Lake]. He and his brother were paddling along in the spring, when all at once his brother let out a warning from the bow of the canoe: "Windigo! Windigo!"

It was a common occurrence, especially in the spring, for someone to see a windigo, which would cause the whole camp to pack up and flee, usually to some island. The superstition originated with a fabled tragedy of long ago. Supposedly a native family had been starving in a hard cold winter and the man, burdened with worry and unable to supply food, went insane and ate up the family. Ever since his death, his evil ghost has been wandering, seeking others to devour. The story paints an ugly picture of this demon who had eaten away his lips in a fit of hunger.

"Well," said the chief's brother, digging in the paddle, "Let's get out of here and tell the people."

The chief was following suit when he remembered what I had said in one of my sermons—a person should always make certain of anything before spreading a false rumour.

So, under his brother's protest, he steered the canoe closer and found it was a tree stump that seemed to rise and bend and move about, caused by fine waves of vapour drawn from the water by the sun. They paddled right up and had a good laugh at themselves, and the annual excitement and fear around the windigo was more or less wiped out for good.

Fishing in the Fall

Always near a full moon toward the end of October when the whitefish would spawn, I went to Eagle Falls. The catch was good and healthy, and fine-tasting food—a great help in supplying the larder. There I enjoyed the companionship of Johnnie Moar, the Hudson's Bay Company manager. Eagle Falls was about eighteen miles more or less east of Little Grand Rapids. Johnnie and I always camped about a mile below the falls. All along that part of the river was the old fishing grounds of the natives and also the Company. I fished closer to the falls and always got more fish than anyone else, but I also lost a net or two.

Johnnie and I would boil the first largest male fish. I know one time the fish must have weighed nearly eight pounds, but this was a ritual with us. We had to eat it all, and we did! Even though fishing was trying and cold work, it was a release from the everyday worries, and I was never more thankful for it than that particular fall.

I used to tease Johnnie and old Alec Keeper because they used homemade nets, floats and rocks. These had some advantage: if the nets got caught on the bottom by rocks and the current, they could still tear them loose. I used the Lake Winnipeg fishermen's corks and leads, and if my net got caught I seldom got it loose again. However, I used the fine twine size 40, while Johnnie and the natives used the heavier twine, size 25, so my nets got torn more easily. But the whitefish has very few fins or protruding parts to get caught by, so it often slips right through the heavier twine, whereas the finer twine gets behind the scales and holds. Anyway, I had lots of fun teasing Johnnie and Alec.

One time I saw Alec (called "The Fishman," for he always outdid all the other natives in fishing) rubbing some native-concocted medicine on his net just before nightfall, when the best catches are made. I told him, "My medicine is stronger than yours." He said, "That's true."

Going home, I had the hardest job carrying nearly one thousand whitefish, slippery and soft, still not frozen, over the long portage at Little Grand. But it was a great and comfortable sight to see those fish at home on the scaffold about ten feet high, all on clean peeled sticks in series of ten, a kind of a deep freeze from which we could help ourselves any time we felt like it all winter. It was also a great satisfaction to be able to help others who were hungry.

This reminds me of one such instance. The Roman Catholic missionary teacher, Mr. Boniface Guimond, passed by our place on his way home from the store. I'd heard that he had a hard time making ends meet. He stopped and said, "Hello. My, you have a lot of nice fish."

I saw the hungry look in his eyes, reached up, and gave him a stick of ten whitefish. He was overcome and finally stuttered, "Mr. Luther, I'll pray that you will be a saint in heaven."

"Not yet!" I replied. "I'd like to stick around a little longer!"

Wood and Food for the Winter

Having Roderick McDonald and his family with us demanded a little more of everything, including more wood. We had to go quite a ways for wood now, for we didn't see why we shouldn't have the best. That we did, and hauled it out mostly quite early before the deep snow. This winter we really piled it up high and long. Grandpa would let no one else cut our wood, so I tried to keep the saw nice and sharp for him. The boys carried it in. Gusti had the very best of wood for her new cookstove, and we were always quite comfortable.

One small cellar was full of fine vegetables, the product of our garden, which seemed to do better and better every year. We had an abundance of potatoes and carrots, also cabbage, and loads of tomatoes. In the meantime I had ordered some hybrids and cherries from the Experimental Farm, some currants, strawberries, and crabapple trees, which all did very well. We also had rhubarb, citrons, cucumbers, and even watermelon. Everything grew well. Watering the garden was the only problem, for we had to carry the pails up from the lake.

Rolf's Death

Perhaps in being so busy with the work among our native peoples, we were remiss in our duty toward our own family, for when we got back, we were again faced with many problems of different kinds. Our oldest son had complained during the winter of sore knees, and begged not to have to walk that mile through snow and cold to school. I thought it was just an excuse not to go, as children often try, so I didn't heed him and made him attend.

When I came home, he again complained about pain in his knees, and we noticed that he looked very pale. I took his temperature and found a 101° fever. We put him to bed. He was now over nine years old and small for his size.

No matter what I tried, day after day, the fever wouldn't go down. Being a firm believer in the healing power of prayer, I prayed, but there was no improvement. I suspected some infection, though I couldn't be certain what it was.

The Forestry heard about it and sent word over that this was their last trip, and they'd be happy to take the boy and me to Lac du Bonnet, a short distance from Winnipeg. I accepted their kind offer, and Rolfie and I both boarded the plane.

It was a rough day. The plane was just like a football in the hands of the elements. I, having had many sleepless nights, became as sick as could be, vomiting until there was no more to come up. Rolfie, thank goodness, was lying down and not sick at all. I have been on rough seas when even some of the crew were seasick, with very few showing up at the dining table, but it never bothered me. This, however, I'll never forget. It was so windy that the pilot had to go farther than he intended, for the waves were too high to land. He said later he was certain he, too, would have been sick if he hadn't been at the controls.

The specialists could do nothing. Rolfie had rheumatic fever and had already progressed so far that the heart was damaged and twice its normal size.

We chartered a plane. It cost us $240, and in one-and-a-half hours we were home again. Three days later our firstborn son, in whom we delighted so much, passed away.

My faith was badly shaken for awhile. In Winnipeg I had had another good friend, Swein Sweinbjornson, who believed in healing prayer and knelt with me to beg the Lord for His healing touch. It was not to be!

Holding that funeral was perhaps the hardest task I ever had to face. We laid Rolfie to rest in the new cemetery near home. For many days I walked there every morning, very early, and knelt down at the tiny grave. I seemed to hear Rolfie's voice trying to comfort me.

No one perhaps felt the loss more keenly than Grandpa, for he had become very fond of Rolfie, being more quiet and not of such a boisterous nature as the other boys. Grandpa had spent more time with him than anyone else, perhaps. We all were so busy busy, never having time for anything. So Grandpa, too, made continued trips to Rolfie's grave, for which we had ordered a stone and an iron fence. It was a lovely spot that Grandpa always loved—the handsome trees, and the good view of the lake with its islands.

Richard Schuetze, the Adopted Son

We still had six boys, because Richard, my sister Verena's son, now became our fully adopted son. His father had forsaken him and his sister and smaller brother, as well as their sickly mother, in a small town in Washington. Richard did very well in Wesley College. He and a Miss Dilabough always were the two top students. When Richard came home during the summer holidays, I initiated him into the rough life of the north, shooting rapids as a bowsman. I have seen his face turn white as a sheet, but he came through with flying colours. It took him a little longer to get used to the pack-strap and being able to carry a big load. Though slight of frame, he became stronger. I have seen him shouldering a 181-pound bag of potatoes from the ground. That summer Richard proved himself over and over again.

Tuberculosis

The winter of 1931 was a trying one in many respects. There was much sickness and many deaths resulted. Especially young girls coming into puberty were struck down with what we called "galloping consumption." It seemed that living in the small, overheated, and overcrowded houses was the principal cause, particularly after a dance, getting overheated and catching colds. You see, not long before we arrived, some half-breeds came up with fiddles and guitars and initiated modern dancing.

I had been like the missionary before me who saw in the drum dances something pagan that had to be done away with. He had taken forcible action and kicked the drum in and said it was of the devil. I felt very much the same way when I heard the first drums. They seemed primeval. As a matter of fact, it made me feel ill at ease; and even later when I became accustomed, I still more or less talked against the drum dance. But as for the modern dances in the small, crowded houses, I used all means to stop them, for I saw the evil they caused. Then when I learned that public dances in overcrowded premises were unlawful, I forbade all such dances during the winter and encouraged the people to go back to their outdoor drum dances if they were done in a thankful mood of happiness.

Deer Lakers and the church they built

Next I contacted the Indian Agent to help the people with lumber, nails, and windows, to build bigger and better houses. They made a provision that no help would be forthcoming unless the house was of a certain size and, I'm glad to say, this improved the situation tremendously. I also told our people to sunbathe—that their ancestors never knew TB until the white man came. There was only one remaining drawback. The most prominent midwife, who had periodical TB with hemorrhages, always administered artificial respiration by sucking and breathing into the baby's mouth. We had a very high mortality rate in newborn babes; oftentimes only two out of ten would live. This improved a great deal when we took the babies away from their mother's breasts and fed them goat's milk. We had lots of it, and the little ones grew into healthy children. Slowly, we were getting somewhere with physical health.

9

"Boys, Boys, Boys"

1932 to 1933

Vacation

As the winter closed in on us and time passed, I noticed that both Gusti and I were not as free of spirit as usual. We were still mourning for little Rolf, who had meant so much to us. We weren't at our best, so I suggested to Gusti that we take a holiday the next summer. I always called her my "wet blanket," for she doused the "fire" quickly by saying we could not do it with all these little ones, and she was expecting again some time in July. However, I kept chipping away at it. In the meantime, Grandpa was fully accustomed to the place. Roderick McDonald and his family were very close to the house, and Fritz, our registered Alsatian, had grown into a lovely big dog of which Grandpa had become very fond.

Finally I won out, and at the end of the school term I prepared for our trip down the river in our canoe, hoping to catch the boat in Berens River. Richard was my bowsman, and then there were the other five boys—Herman almost nine, Ernie seven, Albert five-and-a-half, Daniel three-and-a-half, Gideon just two. We also had Mary Boucher along, one of the chief's daughters, about twelve. So together with Gusti, heavy with child, and myself, it was quite a lively load for a canoe on a treacherous river. But there was no place I was more at home than in a canoe, and we reached Berens River safely, only to learn that the boat had gone by. They couldn't always come in to Berens River if there was a bad wind, for it was a very difficult, crooked, rocky channel of about five miles.

I didn't want to wait, so we took off south toward Winnipeg with our heavily loaded canoe. Gusti was always fearful of rough water and often begged me to land, which was not always possible, since the east shore of Lake Winnipeg is full of reefs, sometimes out from shore. Mary Boucher had no sense of fear and laughed hilariously when a wave splashed over, which made Gusti quite angry.

We camped in a nice little harbour somewhere south of East Doghead. The next day we made the mouth of the Red

Our practically new Packard

River, passed Selkirk, and came to the St. Andrews Locks, which I hadn't given much thought to nor seen for years. When we rounded the bend of the river, I saw the high cement abutments and wondered where to portage my canoe. But I didn't have to wonder long, for as we put-putted along with our old two-horsepower Evinrude, the door of the locks opened. We drove in and they closed. The water rose. I went ashore and entered my name in the logbook.

When the upper doors opened we motored along to Winnipeg, went partly through, then up the Assiniboine River. Many years ago I almost lost my life in this river and saw my partner, an ex-sailor, drown. We came right up to the Granite Rink, which was used as a tourist stopping-place in the summer.

We unloaded our canoe, put up our tent, and made ourselves at home. Then I went around looking for a sec-ondhand car. I had not driven one for eleven years. I found a secondhand Buick which seemed reasonable in price, though not so new anymore. I didn't have too much money with me, so I went to one of my old friends, the secretary of Campbell Brothers and Wilson, and told him what I intended to do.

After he had heard me through, he called, "Charley, come here. I want you to get a nice roomy car for Mr. Schuetze."

This, Charley Edge did—a lovely, practically new, seven-passenger Packard. It is good to have friends like James McKinnon Coutts, whose wisdom made our trip an enjoyable, never-to-be-forgotten one. It was a fine big car and had to be, to accommodate the nine of us and all our bedding, tent, etc. We made very good time. Starting late, we stopped at Brandon and, after four hundred miles of gravel road, which was not too smooth in 1932, we arrived in Morse, Saskatchewan.

Rhoda's Birth

After we put up our tent, Gusti complained that she was uneasy. We expected to be home with her parents near Hanna, Alberta, by noon the next day. However, I had to call a doctor that night and move Gusti into a cabin. I cheered Gusti up by telling her, as before, that we would now have our first girl. She would not believe me. I can still hear her saying, "I can't have anything but boys, boys, boys."

Soon Rhoda, our first girl, was born. Gusti wouldn't believe either the doctor or me! She had to see and make sure it was a girl. After three days I carried her and the baby to the car. Now there were ten of us, and we landed at the Hoffman farm, where we stayed about a week.

The next stopping place was at mother's in Seattle, where we stayed a good while, for mother had a big house with a double garage and some nice fruit trees. We enjoyed the cherries and peaches and Mom's homemade root beer. Then we drove to my sister Irma Boden's in Portland, and after that to Gusti's sister, Tillie Atwater's in Monmouth, Oregon.

We had intended to go farther south to see my brothers Rolf and Frank in California, but time ran out on us. So we

On holiday : Richard, Herman, Mary, Daniel, Gideon,
Albert, and Ernest; in the car, Luther holding Rhoda

visited my sister Gerda Overaa at Port Orchard, and then went home again. In Winnipeg we turned our car back in to Campbell Bros. & Wilson, who sold it for me. We stepped into our canoe and made the 330-odd miles home again. I forgot to mention that when Rhoda was born, we hit the headlines in the newspapers, and Mary Boucher was described as an Indian princess. We were an oddity in those days, but nowadays many families travel and camp.

Back in Little Grand Rapids

Home again. We went back to work and everything was in the old routine again. We felt more refreshed, however, and eager to carry on. Roderick told us that our dog Fritz had been looking for us clear across the lake. Quite a swim, but he loved the water. He always went swimming with the boys, and no matter how they tried to fool him by diving, he was always on top of them when they came up. One thing I had to stop. They used to throw rocks, good-sized ones, and he'd dive and bring them up, but he had ruined a couple of his teeth by doing so.

We had stopped near our old farm and visited a widow and bought some chickens from her, so our farm of animals was enlarged. This meant I had to build a chicken house. Eggs were a luxury up there, especially in the winter, and fresh eggs almost a rarity. But with the chickens we also bought a rooster, who loved nothing better than to attack people with his spurs, thus ruining some of Gusti's stockings.

One day the rooster attacked a young native man down at the beach. He thought it was a great joke and ran as fast as he could down the two hundred or so yards of beach, thinking he had left the rooster way behind. To his amazement, he was right there attacking him again.

We had plenty of vegetables, plenty of milk, butter and cheese—even ice cream, for we had bought one of those hand-turned freezers and had lots of ice. There was fresh fish right in the lake beside us, the net handy, tied to our shore, and now we also had eggs.

Grey Willow Falls

There was never a let-up! Never a dull day! I remember one night I was awakened and called over to a home where a native woman had a very difficult birth and nearly lost her life. She had edema. I worked with her a long time until the baby was born and she was quietly resting. Then her father, an old pagan native, said something I didn't understand and kissed me on the cheek. I still think of that as the greatest accolade I have ever received in all my life. I told her not to have any more babies, but she did, and lost her life while giving birth to another wee daughter. However, that is another story, which will follow later on.

Planes

THE PLANES WERE COMING in more regularly now, for we had the ideal stopping-place. They cached quite a few barrels of gas and oil with us. Sometimes we had as many as four planes at our beach! We had planes from the Royal Air Force, Wings Limited, and Canada Airways, besides private planes with prospectors, etc. One time we had two planes with all the crews and passengers staying with us three days, for a very heavy northwester was blowing and our beach was ideally sheltered. Ted Stull, Jack

Airplanes on the beach at Little Grand Rapids

More, Roy Brown, De Blicky, and many others often stayed with us overnight in the winter when they drained their oil and brought it up to the house to keep it warm. They were real men, those pilots, and did us many favours, too.

I remember a plane with a passenger landing because it had a crippled motor; the piston had pounded right through the cylinder head. Another plane brought in a crew of mechanics and a new motor, which they installed. At the

Postcard showing Hudson's Bay Company Post; from Hudson's Bay Company Archives

table I mentioned to the pilot that I would like to go up with him, but he said, "We are not allowed to take anyone up on a test flight." So I thought that was that.

When I helped finish the job, the pilot got in, waved me in, too, taxied, and took off. After rising to three thousand feet or so, he shifted the controls over to me. I couldn't hear a word he was saying for the roar of the engine. Boy, I hung onto that stick and, apparently by doing so, kind of pushed the stick a wee bit, for at first the pilot waved up with his hand. So I pulled back and up we soared. I steadied down. Then he waved a circle meaning to turn. I used the foot pedals and the stick, but only very gently. I must have made about a ten-mile half circle when he took over the controls. What he did to that plane I never knew, for the whole earth picture became confused. It was slanting and never settled down until he straightened out to land. Everyone came running, wanting to know what was the matter.

"Oh," he said, "that was Mr. Schuetze trying to fly." And that is what they perhaps still believe, if they remember.

Dental Care

Teaching and all the other duties kept me very busy. There was no end of tooth-pulling, for our fame had reached far, and the people came from everywhere. They were all marvellous patients even before I had the anaesthetic and hypodermic needle and Novocain. As a matter of fact, most of them didn't want it. I remember pulling a big molar from a twelve-year-old boy who never gave a sound; just a big tear dropped on his cheek.

One instance I must mention, for I fully believe I was guided by the hand of our Lord. It was in this way: James Keeper, a family man, had what appeared to be lockjaw, for his teeth were clamped so tight he hadn't been able to eat or drink and was slowly starving to death. Upon examining him, I felt around his face and on the left side detected a hard lump well back. I went home and talked it over with the Lord in prayer. Then I went to work and ground myself down a lance-type instrument. Returning to James, I chose the spot, and punctured his cheek and gum. Then I gently squeezed, and blood and matter came out. After putting on a poultice, I went home.

Next day I returned and found to my joy that the man's mouth was open enough so that I could reach in and pull out the second molar of the upper jaw. It was a great success. When I told my mentor, Dr. Roy Bier of Winnipeg, one of Canada's greatest exodontists, he shook his head and said he would've been afraid to do this, for that part of the face is a great nerve centre. He said: "The angels must have guided you."

And so, in spite of difficulties or because of them, our faith grew into an assurance that often we do not realize the wonderful presence and power of our Lord because we, in our modern way of life, turn to every available source of help without turning to Him who said He would always be with us. But when you are away from modern appliances, doctors, scientists and hospitals, you are more or less faced with turning to Him who loved us and gave Himself for us—that is, if we love enough and care enough and are willing enough to help.

Roderick McDonald Leaves for Berens River

In 1933 we were to lose Roderick McDonald who, for family reasons, had to move back to Berens River with his wife and two girls. However, everything was in good shape. The gardens were marvelous, and the piece of land that Richard had cleared had a bumper crop of lovely potatoes, watermelons weighing four and five pounds, and carrots that weighed up to 1–1/4 pounds.

I must mention one amusing incident that happened while Roderick McDonald was still there. He had watered the horses, Bob and Princess, and had left the barn door open, as it was a warm day. The lake was our water trough, and we just chiselled a hole in the ice about a foot wide and three feet long, out of which the animals drank. Roderick came to the dispensary, and while we were talking and looking out the window, I saw Bob coming up the trail toward the house. I told Roderick, "You did not tie Bob. Look!"

"Sure I tied him—he must have undone the tie."

Bob had the rope dragging between his front feet, so Roderick went down, and upon returning, told everyone: "Well, I tied him good this time; he'll never get loose again, or I'll eat my shirt."

"Well," I said, "you had better start eating, for here comes Bob again!"

We missed Roderick and his jokes. He has passed on now to the home prepared for all who love the Lord.

The Church Bell

We had a church now, but no church bell. So we ordered one, hoping to freight it up that winter, for it was too heavy to bring on a canoe. It was shipped by mistake to Berens River, but lo and behold, one day the Forestry plane, an old Vedette, came up and brought that bell right to our shore. What a nice surprise! I must mention that we had the kindest consideration shown to us by the Forestry, experienced many times over, and especially the next year.

We hadn't built a steeple, so now we had to build some kind of structure to hang this bell on. A little south of the church there was a rock. On it we built a strong stand, and hung the bell. It was a wonderful moment when we heard its chimes echoing and re-echoing across the lake, calling our people to worship.

Margaret Strang

Our "princess", Mary Boucher, had gone home from vacation and told of the west coast and seeing the Pacific Ocean, but another girl, nearly her age, took our attention and our pity. No one wanted her; she was kicked from pillar to post. Called Maganegut, her Christian name was Margaret Strang. Her arms were skinny things; her abdomen was bloated almost like a balloon. Filthy and dirty, she had been brought down from the interior.

We took poor Margaret in, but it was quite a while before she responded to our care. Finally she filled out, but she was very backward mentally and quite stubborn. I believe she was the third girl we took in. It was difficult for Gusti, for Margaret had had no schooling and knew very little English; however, she learned fast from the boys, who continually teased her.

The builders of the bell tower; Luther in the front row, far right

10

LIKE FATHER COMING HOME
1933 to 1934

Gusti and the Children Leave for Winnipeg

We were seriously thinking of having Gusti go to town with the whole family, Maganegut included, and also our dog Fritz, for Gusti was again expecting, and we thought of giving the boys a better chance at school. I was beginning to find it quite difficult teaching so many beginners, and mostly natives too. This we finally did, and I took them all to town, where we rented a house on Lansdowne Avenue.

It was hard to say good-bye, and it was to be very lonely and quite difficult to keep house, teach, and do all the other things besides. We were gratified with the school reports later on, proving to us that we had given our boys a good sound foundation, for all did very well. Both Herman and Ernie held first place in their respective classes in the Luxton School.

And so the work went on, with pleas for help of every sort that you can imagine. We had to be a bit stern at times. However, as one man, Omeme (Pigeon Dunsford), said when the whole dispensary was full, "It is just like our father coming home when we were children." They depended on us and in their way loved us.

If it was hard on me, it was also hard on Gusti. This was the first time in our married life that she was all on her own with five boys, a wee baby, and a native girl to look after. She found it very hard. Grandpa had gone down to my brother Rodi's in Berens River for a visit, and Richard and I were alone. I had left a goodly sum of money with Gusti, figuring it would last her until spring. However, she found it melting away fast, what with dentist bills, etc., so she was worried. She let me know about it; therefore I made up my mind that by Christmas I would leave Richard in charge and go to town. I got a ride down with one of the teams as far as Bloodvein, walked over to Matheson Island (Snake Island as we knew it), and hired a dog team to Fisher River, where I boarded a train. We were a happy, reunited family that Christmas.

Margaret Strang (Maganegut) with Rhoda and Fritz in Winnipeg, 1933

The Twins Are Born in Winnipeg

On January 15th, about two in the morning, Gusti told me she was in pain. I phoned here and there for a taxi but couldn't get one. The temperature was around thirty below zero. Finally I ran down to Main Street and managed to flag one, and at 5:00 a.m. twin girls were born by the use of instruments. They looked so tiny and cute, like two little dolls. Gusti never saw them both alive, for the biggest one passed on the next morning. After seven days I took Gusti home. Though she weighed 160-odd pounds, the joy of having her home again made her seem light as a feather as I carried her up the stairs to our bedroom. Tiny Elizabeth weighed only about three pounds, and could only make a noise like a mouse's squeak. However, she grew up into a good husky woman.

Returning Home Without Herman and Ernie

It was time to get back to my work. No one wanted to stay behind, but we boarded Herman and Ernie with the Mathesons (Mr. Matheson was a descendant of Bishop Matheson) and chartered a plane from Lac du Bonnet. On the flight before ours they burned out the wiring heating the plane, so we had to wait there overnight for another one. We stayed in the only big room left in the hotel. Unfortunately it was right over the beer parlour, and never in my life have I heard such vile language.

Next morning we found that we had to board a Junkers freight plane that wasn't heated. There were sleigh dogs going out on that plane so I protested, saying I had paid for a chartered plane and would not put my family together with vicious dogs. Besides, Fritz was with us. Finally we were off. It was a rough ride. Margaret started first and before you knew it, all the children were vomiting, except the baby. When we finally landed at Little Grand it was cold, and most of the children froze their cheeks or noses on the way up to the house. So we were all together again—now six boys and two girls, Margaret, Mom, and I. Eleven of us. Grandpa was to be back later.

Death of Pikangikum Missionary, James Kirkness

Another great sorrow gripped me when I found out that the Pikangikum natives had brought down their beloved missionary's body all the way by dogsled, nearly two hundred miles, which they had to travel back again, without asking for any pay whatsoever. I remembered how coming down they often used to drop a deer or some game in front of Jimmy's tent when he was holidaying at our place. So Jim's work was over.[14]

He was a quiet, kindly man with infinite patience in his teachings and interpretation of the Gospel. You always saw him with his bulky Cree Bible. He had helped me a lot the short time he stayed in Little Grand, for he was married to one of our native women, and had a real understanding of the workings of the native mind. It was a great loss, although the church at large or at headquarters would hardly notice it, for Jimmy was not a man who made himself known. You had to seek him out and then you found pure gold.

By this time the frost was several feet deep, so it was hard digging, but we laid his earthly remains to rest near our son's grave. When we returned for a visit in 1960, we wouldn't have known the grave if one of my former pupils hadn't shown it. We were shocked to see that it, as everything else on the grounds, was sadly neglected.

Richard Goes to Pikangikum

Coming back, we were concerned with Pikangikum. We didn't have any contact with the Presbytery nor the Home Mission Board, so we took it upon ourselves and sent Richard up. He was tried on that trip, for I hired Sasho and his dog team, but Richard was nimble on his feet and proved himself. They made it to Pikangikum in record time. It was a good move for the people, and they soon more or less

Richard Schuetze, c. 1939

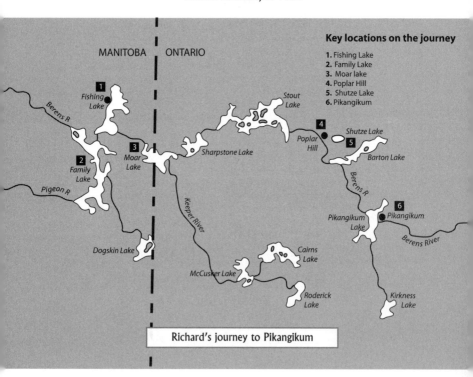

Richard's journey to Pikangikum

adopted him. The Home Mission okayed the move, and Richard became the missionary teacher at Pikangikum. He soon mastered their language and was one of them.

Richard was the only white person there, so he had no companionship in kind. This bothered me, but he was now twenty-two years old and well broken in the way of life in the interior—that is, he knew how to fish, pack across portages, cook at open fires, snowshoe, handle an axe, and so forth. The people soon called him by no other name than Nitchience, meaning our little friend. That was the name he was soon known by everywhere.

[Excerpts from Richard Schuetze's taped memoirs of his time at Little Grand Rapids are contained in Appendix B.]

Bringing the Kirkness Family to Berens River

In the spring, Mrs. Kirkness and the three girls came down by canoe, and after a while Gusti and I took them down to Berens River. They had quite a bit of baggage, but we shot many of the more difficult rapids anyway, and of one I must tell, for I am particularly proud of Gusti's part in it. It was at the Big Conjuring Falls. We sometimes threw a big log into the water above the falls on the south side, for we were told that nothing ever comes out. Being skeptical, we tried it. Well, the logs never came up again.

Above the falls, the water is swift and treacherous. When it's high you can hug the shore fairly closely, although it is all boulders, and make a little cove where you have only a very short liftover of canoe and freight. We were being raced by Sinnigan and two other natives going down. We caught up with them on a long quiet stretch of about five miles, as we had a faster motor. However, they got ahead of us on the portages, since there were three of them to carry the canoe and freight. On this day, the water above the falls was quite low, so if I wanted to make that short portage at the cove and beat Sinnigan, I had to go out almost in the middle of the stream and then, just a short distance from the falls, make a quick and desperate strike across the strong current for the little bay. I couldn't use the engine, as the stream was all boulders, nor could I go close for fear of hitting a boulder and tipping over. I stood up, took a general survey of the thing, and decided we could make it if Gusti did her part—and we did!

While we were making the short portage now well ahead of Sinnigan and his crew, he came over and had a look at it. I don't know what he thought but I felt heady, for here a husband and wife had pulled together and accomplished a

Christmas gifts arrive from Winnipeg for the children

great task. I was thankful and at the same time thought what a great pity that so many married couples never learn to work together as a team and thus victoriously overcome great obstacles. We were never caught up again, and got to Berens River in good time for the boat that was to take Jimmy's family to Norway House. We have never seen them again, with the exception of Lucy, who is married in Berens River. We hope they are well.

11

The Will to Die
1934 to 1935

Setting a Broken Leg

The years 1934 and 1935 slipped by quickly. Oh, many things happened. For one, Joe Potvin joined our Church and became my right hand man as interpreter and helper in all work.[15] He was an expert with a scythe and one of my main companions on the hay ground.

One day I had a call from the people at the Roman Catholic Mission. A boy there, one of the Dunsfords, about thirteen years of age, had broken his leg very badly two or three days earlier. They were at their wits' end. Well, I took Joe with me and it was a good thing I did. It was a very bad break—a compound fracture, the one bone sticking right out near the calf. The leg was dirty and full of clotted blood. I cleaned it up thoroughly then made splints, many of them. I told Joe to hold the boy's shoulders, and took the foot and pulled. I was extremely strong (I had once bested a threshing crew of nearly twenty men in weightlifting on a platform scale by lifting all the weights, 1,300 pounds easily), and I had to use all that strength to get the bone back in, place the two broken parts together, and put on the splints, praying all the time for the Lord's help. We finally had the leg well bandaged and seemingly everything in place. The boy had never uttered a sound as his mother wiped great drops of sweat from his forehead.

That night I couldn't sleep, thinking of that boy's leg. I was afraid of an infection, gangrene or what have you. In the morning I cut up a whole lot of cardboard splints and with Joe went over to see the boy. He had had a comfortable night. I took all the splints off, washed out the wound with antiseptics, then put on the cardboard splints, always cutting out a hole at the place of the wound. Finally I put the bandages back on, leaving the wound open.

Every day I went over and washed it, and prayed for a plane to come. A Forestry plane finally arrived and took the boy to town. The receiving nurse was amazed and asked the pilot, "What a wonderful job, did you do that?" He said he wished he could have said yes, for she was such a pretty nurse.

Carl Eugen Felix Schuetze 1856-1934

Some years later I met a doctor on the boat who asked me where I was from. "Little Grand Rapids," I told him. "Well," he said, "that is the place from which we received a patient a few years ago, and his leg was so perfectly set when we took the X-ray, we had to do nothing but put the cast on." I didn't tell him I was that man, for the credit belongs to the Lord who helped and inspired me, for I depended on Him.

Sports at Little Grand Rapids

I must tell of some of our sports activities. We always enjoyed softball games on the Hudson's Bay grounds, and hockey in the bay at our place. I bought skis for all the boys from the smallest to the biggest.

One day we had with us some Norwegian trappers, old acquaintances and friends of ours. They saw the skis and right away tried them on. Our house was up on quite a hill.

The road down was packed solid, and on the shore the ice on the boulders had formed a kind of bank. No one was able to make it down that hill, rise suddenly at the bank, and get over it through the air to land on the frozen lake. They all tried and all fell at the last obstacle.

So one of them went up to coax Mom to come and try to ski down. She was in a dress, cooking dinner. I told her not to, but she isn't always obedient, forgetting that when she married me she promised to honour and

Jean McConnell on skis, 1938
[See chapter 14]

obey me. To everyone's surprise, she made it without falling, and she had never been on skis before!

Hockey was always popular, but not everyone was willing to shovel snow and keep the rink clean. For a while I had a Swiss with me by the name of Geiger.[16] He was a good skater and could jump a whole row of boxes or barrels without falling.

End of the Chickens

Our poultry farm ended suddenly. One morning, in the fall, I believe, Fritz was barking angrily. A native dog had managed to get through the little hole made for the chickens to go in and out. It was usually closed at night, but someone had left it open. There was a dog inside who wanted out, but was trapped, either because he had eaten too much or because of Fritz.

When Gusti saw the dog, she went back to the house, got the gun, and shot him. Generally she is slow and deliberate, but this time she was quick in action, for the dog had killed practically all the chickens, heaped them up in a pile for future use, and covered them as best he could. When Gusti took the pile apart she found several that weren't dead. That was the end of our chicken ranch, and it was a good thing, for we had good use for that chicken house later on.

Miss Mosel and the School

Now winter was drawing nigh and plans had to be made. Who was to drive the second team?[17] The natives were afraid of horses, looking upon them as overgrown dogs. I am told the Cree word for horse, Atim, suggested "big dog." So there was nothing to do but send for a teacher, and it was Miss Mary Mosel who came out. She was a certified teacher and a good one, a kindly, friendly young person. I paid her the going salary out of my own pocket, and we didn't charge her for board. We never charged anyone. Our house was always open and free to all who came.

When I was advised of the teacher's arrival by boat, I took two native boys with me, Moose Boucher and Sesheewap (David Eaglestick), who were experts on the river. By this time I had acquired an eight-horsepower Evinrude that could really churn up the waters. We made it down in a day—108 miles and some 52 rapids and falls, not a mean feat!

Miss Mosel had never been away from home, and she shed a few tears on arrival by boat in a strange place. I jollied her up, and the next morning we left early, hoping to make it in two days. We did make good time, and camped above the Old Fort Falls. I put up our mosquito bar for Miss Mosel on the hill, partly under some trees. Moose and David retired farther into the bush.

It was getting dark, and I was on the verge of falling asleep near the shore where I had made my bed, when I heard, "Mr. Schuetze! Mr. Schuetze!"

I hastened up the hill. Miss Mosel was very agitated, saying she was afraid of the Indians. I tried to comfort her but to no avail. "Can't you come up and sleep with me, please, please?" There was lots of room in the mosquito bar (our whole family used to sleep in it), so I brought up my bedding and soon we were both asleep.

We arrived early in Little Grand Rapids. Miss Mosel quickly became a cherished part of our household. I never tried to find out if Moose and David had seen me enter Miss Mosel's sleeping quarters and never heard anything about it. We only hope and trust that Miss Mosel, wherever she is, is happy and content, for she certainly made a wonderful contribution to the work of our school and our mission. Very soon the classroom, for the first time, was gaily decorated with coloured cutouts of birds, flowers, plants, trees, houses, children playing—all neatly pasted on white cardboard. It was a pleasure to visit the school and notice the children's reaction, especially the girls, to such a winsome teacher. However, there were to be serious repercussions later on from unexpected quarters.

It was nice to be free to look after the people, as well as

to have more time to spend on preparation for the building of a church. Often at school we had to rush off and leave the classroom in charge of some older pupil when someone was injured or needed immediate help.

Grandpa's Death

The lake waters were high in 1934, inundating much of our usual hay ground, so I had to look for higher ground. I heard of a little lake about four miles east of us, closed in on all sides. It was a very warm place, with no breeze to cool it, so when we found a little creek where we were cutting, we used to jump in and out, and continue our work. It was a great relief. This lake was not visible from Family Lake. I had to cut a portage wide enough to allow a load of hay to go through.

In the meantime, Grandpa had taken to his bed. He had a cold and was not feeling so good. I went over to the Hudson's Bay and got him some cigars and a bottle of Three Star Hennessy. He used to make his own cigarettes, but had given that up. Gusti made them for him once in a while, but he didn't want either of these things now, and I was worried. But I had to go and cut that trail, leaving before daylight and coming back after dark.

I finally finished and was elated that my worries were now over, for I visualized myself driving up the next day and bringing back some of this nice green upland hay. Arriving home, as always I liked to surprise and scare someone. It was Gusti who came to the door and dealt me a blow that almost sunk me: "Sh! Sh!" she said, "Grandpa is gone."

My dad, for whom I had had very little time, being so busy—just eat and run, work, and work—it broke me! He had been a good dad.

Carl Eugen Schuetze was a well-educated man, a chartered accountant in Berlin. Finding that he didn't like inside work, he became a civil engineer in 1886 and moved to Brazil with his bride. The Brazilian government under Don Pedro was offering great tracts of land to worthy settlers.

However, my mother couldn't stand the wilderness, for Dad often had to go to town and leave her alone with their dog, a setter, who growled at nights when wild animals prowled around. So Mom, a strong-willed woman, laid down the law, and they moved to the town of Joinville. It had a population of several thousand, but there wasn't one dentist. So Dad went back to Germany and studied dentistry, while Mom opened up a dry goods store and gave sewing lessons. When Dad returned, he opened up his dental parlour and traveled by horseback far and wide to relieve people's miseries. He became an expert dental mechanic. (Mother, in later years, often tried to get a new set of teeth made in Winnipeg, but always went back to the set Dad had made.) Then malaria overtook him, and upon doctor's orders he came to Canada and settled down on a farm.

I can never remember Dad chastising any one of us seven children, but he did take us in his study and talk to us, sometimes for half an hour, explaining things. I would sooner have taken a spanking from Mom, for it was fast over with.

But now he was gone, and I had to make the coffin and hold his funeral. That was another hard thing to do, but we found there is no truer word than found in the good Book: "My strength is sufficient unto thee." We learned what the Psalmist found, that the Lord is the strength of my life.

The loss was doubly hard when we found a Chalmers Journal opened at an article entitled, "The Will to Die," which explained cases of exercised willpower to die. One of them, I remember, happened in India. Grandpa passed away on December 4th, 1934, just a few days short of his 78th birthday. And so we had two loved ones in the Little Grand Rapids United Church Cemetery.

It was that same winter when Mrs. J. Keeper, whose life we were once privileged to save, gave birth to another child and died. Another little girl in a family of three girls and a father—what could we do? We took the newborn baby home, raised her on goat's milk, and named her Patricia. She grew up to be a healthy, stout, and strong girl, and we grew quite fond of her. So now we had four girls, two of our own and two of native birth.

The Family Takes a Tumble

Rhoda, Gusti, and baby Patricia

The church was a simple one, with no pews or seats, just boards with boxes and blocks of wood under them. An amusing incident happened in one of our services. Our family (all of them, and I do mean all, for Gusti always had everyone there from the baby up) always sat on one of the first seats on the west side. I was ready to begin the service when Miss Mosel arrived. Being quite stout, when she plunked herself down, crack went the board, tumbling everyone to the floor. It was such a comical sight, but I had to keep from smiling. I guess it was the hardest time I ever had to do this, excepting one that happened in that same church later on.

12

WAITING UPON THE GREAT SPIRIT
1935 to 1936

Canoeing

Little Grand Rapids and Family Lake are very beautiful in summer and winter. We have often missed that sandy beach. The lake's nice soft water, especially in the summertime, caresses in its embrace. I did love to swim in it. One day it was a bit windy. There were some waves, but I decided to swim across to the island about half a mile away. I was about halfway when I saw Gusti coming along in the small canoe. She was worried about me, and I was worried about her. When she caught up I gave her a scolding, for she had never travelled alone in a canoe and it was quite rough. So when we reached the island, I entered the canoe and took over on the way back.

Gusti became quite a proficient bowsman in my canoe, and I shot many very difficult rapids with her. There was one place where she obeyed me swiftly and without hesitation, for she knew that it could mean death if she didn't.

One year at the annual festivities there were canoe races—one for the women in small canoes, two women to a canoe. They were all ready to go when Soap (Mrs. Kittigas) came and asked my wife if she would be her partner. I said, "Go ahead," and to my surprise, they came in first.

Our RCMP constable didn't do so well at all. The course for men was to go out about half a mile, then turn around an anchored canoe and come back home to the starting point. Two of my pupils—William Keeper was the captain—came in first as the constable and his partner were just rounding the halfway mark. This, of course, amused the natives very much, as they always got a great kick out of beating the white man.

My brother Rodi and I used to travel hundreds of miles by paddle, and were often tried by many natives in their canoes. But we were never beaten, empty or loaded, perhaps because we took a leaf out of the natives' book—we despised the factory-made paddles as toys and always made our own with much longer blades. Our paddles never let us down under any circumstances. And it was the same with snowshoes. We used

Treaty party: RCMP Constable Putnam, Luther Schuetze, and Indian Agent Irwin

to make our own until we had the exact model that suited us best. That is why we were respected by the natives, and that is why my teaching was more readily accepted, for somehow they sensed that we knew what we were talking about.

The Anishinabe Character and Tradition

Mrs. Sasho Keeper and her children, with the baby in her tikinagan (baby carrier)

These Anishinabe natives, often described by writers as black-hearted and stiff-necked people, were not so at all. When we got to know them, we found them to be kind-hearted and generous. They would do anything for a person, oftentimes many things that would put a white man to shame. They knew they were being victimized in various ways, and that is why they were suspicious of all white men. They were of me, too, but they came to love us, and when we made a trip up there after thirty years' absence, we received the most royal welcome we have ever received in our whole lives.

The native people have often been christened with Christian names, but they still hang onto their native names, which often are very embarrassing if translated into the English language. I found that out to my sorrow when I started teaching. I called some of the bigger girls by their native names, and later was told what they meant. Some of them, to say the least, were very embarrassing, but being the so-called "Nature's children," the natives thought nothing of it. They often named their children after certain peculiarities. For instance, if a little baby persisted in sticking out some part of her or his anatomy, that is what the child was called. More often they named them after animals such as fox, fisher, deer, and so on. I was told that the boys had the privilege of changing their names when they reached maturity.

Along the Pigeon River I once saw huge bunches of branches on the tops of scrub trees and willows, and I was told that the young men had gone and built this so-called huge nest where they would lie without food or water, night and day if necessary, until the Great Spirit came and gave them a name. This was no longer practised after we came, but I thought it was quite an idea to be lifted up from the ground and away from all earthly impact, to wait upon the Great Spirit to meet them there.

They had two names for the God they believed in, Manitou and Kitche Achshak (Great Spirit). However, there were many more spirits. Wiskacheck was a benign spirit, but the others were mostly evil ones. I remember at one time, one of the conjurers came around the point with his canoe to the mission and asked me to accompany him across the lake. I thought he wanted me to go with him in his canoe, but no, he wanted me to accompany him closely with my canoe, for he was afraid of one of the water spirits. He was so agitated that I had to comply with his request, feeling very foolish about it.

Here I must record what Dave Donaldson and I once did, on our trip to Pikangikum. Before coming to a portage, not far from Pikangikum, we noticed a round stone about two feet in diameter placed on a point jutting out below the falls. We went over to inspect it and found that it represented an image of some kind, for behind it on the flat rock were placed offerings of many kinds—dishes, fish-hooks, tobacco, and many other articles. So we presumed this was the replica of a god of some kind, who afforded protection upon the waters if an offering was made to him. In our fervour, we rolled the stone off its pedestal and into the water, and thought no more of it.

Many years later we heard that Fred Moar (a son of Johnnie Moar and an outpost manager for the Hudson's Bay

Company) came along and found the water very low and the round stone within easy reach. Having heard that the old natives were very much perturbed by the disappearance of their idol, he and his men got to work and rolled it on to a canvas then dragged it up to its former position. For all I know it still sits there, but I believe it's no longer of any significance, for the Pikangikum people, under the tutorship of Jimmy Kirkness and Richard, embraced Christianity wholeheartedly.

More Ailments

Gusti and I were out somewhere when a stranger was brought to the mission by some natives in the afternoon. He was badly swollen all over, and everyone was afraid of some terrible disease. Trembling, Miss Mosel let him in where we had our medical supplies, and when we came home she told us that he was a Roman Catholic, but the R.C. Mission had refused him shelter. So he came to us, and she didn't know what to do. I calmed her down, then took the man inside and examined him. He was terribly swollen on all his extremities, so I told him I'd see that he got down to Berens River and to the boat.

The next day I hired two of our younger men and gave them one of my older canoes, though strong in the bottom, stripped with five oak keels. I told them to leave the man in at every portage, for he couldn't walk, and to pull the canoe over the portages. This they did, and got him safely down. During the night he had stayed with us, Miss Mosel was very nervous and wanted protection, and after the man left I had to burn our outhouse and build a new one, for everyone thought it was a terrible disease. This man's partner had died from it in the woods, and the body was in such a terrible state that the RCMP burned it. Later on we received a grateful letter from the man, saying he was completely recovered, that it was only some vitamin deficiency.

Flying with the Treaty Party

In the meantime, I had become an interpreter in great demand, and had to fly around with the treaty party.[18] I had the privilege of seeing Richard for the first time since we sent him to Pikangikum to replace the deceased Jimmy Kirkness.

We had an outdoor service there on Sunday. Richard, who had become quite fluent in reading the Cree syllabics, read the lesson, and I brought the message. I doubt if any one of the whole Pikangikum reserve was missing. It was a grand sight. They all assembled in front of the mission house, and we had as our choir the whole staff of the treaty party, the two pilots of the Royal Air Force planes, the two mechanics of the same, our lady doctor, RCMP Constable Putnam, Indian Agent Mr. Andrew Irwin, and the clerk Frank Lockhard. It was an unforgettable time, with the lake as a splendid background, and the woods on each side as the frame!

Here I must state that in all my experience of labour among our natives, which takes in twenty-three years, I have never seen an Indian agent who could compare with

Outdoor service at Pikangikum, treaty time

Dr. Krause examining child at Sandy Lake, treaty time

Mr. Irwin. He had the whole welfare of the native people so much on his heart that he was willing to lay his position on the line with a good chance of losing it, yet he did not hesitate. He was the best—a thorough, convinced Christian.

I got so accustomed to flying with the Royal Air Force that I lost all fear of flying. They were so competent and so relaxed. From Pikangikum we flew to Deer Lake, and then to Sandy Lake, where we had been instrumental in placing the bigger part of the Deer Lakers. The Deer Lake country had been badly burned, and the fish and game were not so plentiful anymore, whereas Sandy Lake offered more of an agricultural possibility. There, also, some of that noble fish, the inland sturgeon, could be had.

From there we flew toward James Bay. I believe the Crane River people lived there. When we landed at the designated place, the two planes slid gently onto the sandy beach. There was a good-sized group of men standing there. They all looked solemn, not a smile on their faces (unlike the Deer Lakers), and not a woman or child to be seen. I greeted them in the Anishinabe tongue, and it was just like the sun coming up over the horizon, such a change came over all their faces. As I stood on the pontoon of the plane, I was extremely thankful when I

Miss Mosel with treaty party at Little Grand Rapids

heard the chief's welcome. I have never forgotten the first thing he said: "I am so glad that you have brought someone along who speaks our language!"

I have often since thought about the Bible story of the tower of Babel—how men tried to reach heaven. You might say they tried to reach higher qualities of life the wrong way

Treaty party in school at Little Grand Rapids; Anishinabe men with Luther and Constable Putnam on platform

and became utterly confused. They have never been able to understand one another since, and have not been able to realize the really high standards of life for which man has been created, because they are seeking the wrong way by not seeking it in the mark of the high calling of Christ, our Lord.

These people had never been contacted or received into treaty. So we got busy taking census. The first snag was when we ran into a man who had two wives. The man told only me, so after he had given the Indian agent his name, and the names of one woman and the children, then one more woman, everyone—the agent, the clerk, Constable Putnam—looked confused. So I said, "The man is trying to tell you that he has two wives."

"That is against the law," burst out the Constable.

"Well, what can you do about it?" I asked.

"Nothing," he replied.

U.C. Mission; Royal Air Force planes on beach

These people had lived by themselves and were a law unto themselves. The brand new dollar bills were given and received for the first time, but the doctor was still very busy, mostly with the children, so we stayed a while. When we left, I again thought how strange—here is a people of our own nation, right on our doorstep, completely forgotten and neglected by us, yet we send missionaries to foreign lands and make much to-do about it, forgetting that the beginning of success for the Gospel lies in the words of our Saviour: "Beginning at Jerusalem."

On the way home, our pilot asked me if I would like to salute our home, and I said yes.

They peeled off at about five thousand feet and zoomed down. I thought for sure he was going to hit the stovepipe that was our chimney. It was a grand experience in July of that year.

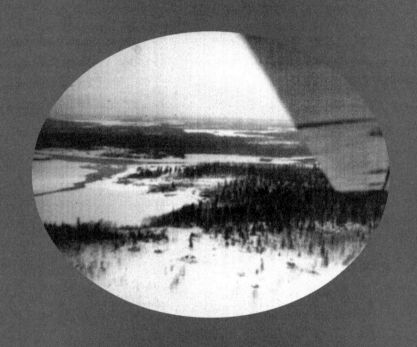

13

AN AIRPLANE HALO

1936 to 1937

Gold Fever

Richard and I were startled one summer, and Gusti too, I guess. A reliable prospector named Middleton came over and told us that he had found gold in the vicinity of Little Grand. He had staked all that he could for his company and for himself, and believed that people who lived in the district should have first opportunity, and that as soon as he went out the planes would come buzzing in, and the place would be overrun with prospectors. Richard and I talked it over. I was never enthusiastic about gold or money, as far as that goes, but we thought of the good we could do in building decent schools, etc. So we had a look at it, and the next day went out with Mr. Middleton and Fred Moar. Mr. Middleton showed us how to stake the claims. I still remember that I had a good laugh at Fred, for as we were staking his claim, we found loads of good-sized golden berries. We didn't know their names, so we called them "banadan berries." I told him, "You are a lucky one, for gold sure must be plentiful here, and not far down—just look at the lovely golden colour of these berries."

Sure enough, a few days later planes were buzzing around and there was great excitement. However, it all came to nothing. The assay showed there was gold all right, but the cost of production would be prohibitive for mining. So the bubble burst, and we were again on a normal, even keel in our community.

Church Services

Our services were well attended, you might say, when over a quarter of the whole population attended. At that time the population of Little Grand was near the two hundred mark. One Sunday we were agreeably surprised when over a dozen white men attended with Jock Stewart, the new Hudson's Bay manager. They were university students out on a survey. They came over to worship with us, for which we were very grateful. As a general rule, the white

Winter view from above U.C. Mission, looking towards open water near H.B. Co. Post where Luther travelled to get the mail

man does not set a very good example before our natives, but rather, the contrary. This makes the missionary's work all the harder, often destroying much of months' and years' painstaking work in a few careless moments of liquor, obscene language, and immorality, sometimes coming from people you never would have suspected.

In the summer, our people mostly moved to the islands that lay in the bay, just below where the Little Grand Rapids Falls current joins Family Lake. It was cooler there, and they were closer to the stores. It often was very hot in midsummer when the granite rock reflected the sun's heat. Then we would hold our services in the evening on the most populated island, which was generally the closest to the Hudson's Bay grounds.

These were blessed occasions, and often reminded us of our Lord's ministry along Lake Galilee, when the waves gently lapped against the shore under a nice breeze. There were hardly ever any mosquitoes. Our only trouble, once in a while, would be dogs that had no regard for our service, going around wherever they pleased. But mostly it was just grand.

Trips to Pauingassi

It was not always peaceful in my services among the natives of Pauingassi with their babies crying. During one winter service I remember rabbits hanging over the stove, thawing out, then falling on the hot surface, their singed hair fouling up the air.

The trip up there in winter was made generally on foot, in the company of a few natives. They tried me again and again in running. It was only about ten miles, but it took all I had, for I was much heavier than any of them—187 pounds when I was down to my running form. But often I'd put on an extra pound or two, and on those occasions I really regretted it.

But we enjoyed it all. There was a really free kind of atmosphere, free from all theological decorations or ecclesiastical dogma. It was just plain down-to-earth life, trying to reach out and touch the hem of the Saviour's garment to be made whole.

A Drastic Remedy for a Cold

By now we had a new Hudson's Bay manager, for Johnnie Moar had moved to Berens River and built himself a nice house near the point on the south side of the bay.[19] Mr. and Mrs. Jock Stewart

Johnnie Moar at Berens River

were very nice people and had no family. We saw them quite often in church, as well as at the fort and at our home. While they were there, something happened that I have never forgotten. I had been teaching and had a dreadful cold and was just looking forward to Friday afternoon. I always started my school punctually at 9:00 a.m. and never let any one go until 4:00. I had swallowed ten aspirins that day, and when it finally ended, I went home to bed. Gusti put a mustard plaster on my chest and I felt a bit better.

This was in February, and we had had no mail for a long time. So when the mail plane came and flew over our house and landed at the Hudson's Bay, we knew that some of our long-awaited mail would be there. Against Gusti's protest, I got up that Saturday morning and dressed to get the mail. It was a difficult way, for the falls stayed open all winter, and below there was a lot of open water and unsafe ice for a mile or so, depending on the frosts. We had to go along a path through the woods until we came to a place of open water below the falls, where there would be a canoe with a paddle. We'd paddle across, leave the canoe, and walk over.

When I got to this place the canoe was there, correctly tipped over so it wouldn't gather any snow, but when I turned it up there was no paddle! Looking up the bank, I saw the paddle standing against a tree. I went to get it, and just when I reached, heard a noise. Looking around, I saw the canoe sliding into the current. Racing down, but too late, I jumped into the water after the canoe and brought it back to shore. So I paddled over, only to find the store closed. I knocked at the kitchen door and Mrs. Stewart let me in. She threw up her arms and said, "Why, you are soaking wet; let me get you some of Jock's underwear."

I told her, "It will be much too small for me, Mrs. Stewart, but I'm sorry to mess up your kitchen." The water was just dripping off me.

"Oh, that's nothing," she said, "I have to scrub today, anyway—it's Saturday."

So I took my mail and went back home. Well did I get scolded, Gusti telling me that I would catch pneumonia, for I'd had it pretty bad before.

The reason I tell this story is this: the cold that I couldn't shake all week had completely gone! I woke up on Sunday morning fit as a fiddle, not a speck of hoarseness or cough or fever. When I asked Dr. Krause about it, she said the shock of the ice-cold water had prompted the blood corpuscles to throw all the cold germs right out of the pores. However, I wouldn't recommend it as a sure cure. Ninety-odd percent would have disastrous results. So I found a cure for colds, but apparently it's not foolproof.

Eye Trouble

This was to be a memorable winter. For one thing, I noticed I was having difficulty with my eyes. I was always proud of them because I could spot game quicker than almost anybody else, including natives. I noticed a white tissue slowly spreading over my eyes, working its way towards the pupils. So when Easter came and a plane stopped at the mission for gas and lunch, the pilot suggested that I go along. Unconsciously he did me a great service, for I would have been incurably blind now for over thirty years.

As soon as I got to town, I consulted our friend Dr. Krause, the foremost surgeon in the clinic. She looked at my eyes and said, "You need an operation at once."

"Well, go ahead," I told her.

She laughed and said, "There is only one or two in the whole of Winnipeg who can do that."

The surgeon, Dr. H.G. Grieve, confirmed Dr. Krause's report that I must have an immediate operation on both eyes. He explained to me that this tissue (I believe he called it "ptyrigium") is a scar tissue that has been caused by continued injury to the eyes, as often happens to people in the barren north when the strong winds pelt the eyeball with fine particles of snow. This tissue gradually spreads, destroying everything underneath, and once it goes over the eyeball, sight is lost forever. He said I had double scar tissue on the one eye, and single on the other, both dangerously close to the pupil. That I had come in was very fortunate. He also explained that this tissue, being a part of the eye, could not be taken off, but only peeled down and grafted on below the eyeball. I was considerably shaken but extremely thankful that I had come to Winnipeg.

In the hospital there was an amusing incident. I had to disrobe and put on the hospital shirt, then climb on a wagon that a slight, elderly chap pushed toward the elevator. There was a bit of a rise on the floor and he got stuck momentarily. I told him to lie on the wagon and I'd push it up, but he would have none of it. In the operating room some of the nurses wanted to strap me in. The doctor told them, "Never mind. This fellow could break all of them. We just have to trust him."

Then came the operation: freezing the eye, peeling down the tissue, then sewing it on. I had three stitches in one eye and two in the other. Lying there bandaged, I was a real weeping Jeremiah for weeks afterward, but the most impatient patient the hospital ever had. They fed me like a babe, and when I protested and said, "Just give me the food and I can feed myself," I was told, "No, you must be one of the bossy kind. Here you do just as you are told."

So there I lay, a big husky chap with lots to do. Finally, after several days the nurse told the doctor that I was restless to get going, so he came in and took the bandage off. "Can you see that light?" he asked. I answered, "Yes, but it is only like a red strawberry to me."

What a relief to get out, though I was very nearly killed stepping onto Portage Avenue right in front of a car that I didn't see. Luckily the brakes were good, and I just got knocked down. I was more careful after that.

A week or so later, Dr. Grieve took the stitches out and I felt much better, but I was still weeping away. Even so, on

the way home by plane, with Roy Brown flying above the clouds in the sunshine, I saw a sight never to be forgotten. We were flying northeast toward Little Grand when all at once on the clouds there was a perfect rainbow circle, and within the circle was the perfect silhouette of our plane. Roy called it an "airplane halo." I dug for my camera to take a picture, but it was too late. Approaching home I took several pictures of our mission ground that turned out very well.

Naturally I was glad to be back home. Richard was teaching in my place and Gusti had held some services, funeral and otherwise. We were all thankful for the providence that God, through this pilot and the surgeon, had saved my eyesight.

The end of an era—the last birch bark canoe built at
Little Grand Rapids by an Anishinabe canoe builder

14

THE RED VELVET PULPIT AND THE CONJURING TENT

1937 to 1938

The Thorwaldsons and Jean McConnell Arrive

A new family of Icelandic origin came to Little Grand Rapids. We invited the Thorwaldsons to make their home on the western point of the church property. This they did, and we found them very congenial and pleasant neighbours. Their three young girls made a pleasant company for our children, and we all grew very fond of Marno, of his wife Ingeborg, and their daughters—Margaret, Bernice, and Shirley. Marno, by the way, is a brother of Senator Thorwaldson.[20]

That same fall we met Jean McConnell, a very pleasant and fine daughter of the Rev. McConnell of the United Church at Little Britain, on the boat. She had a first-class certificate as a teacher. We asked her if she would come up to Little Grand and teach for us. She said she would.

So we got busy and converted our chicken house, with its nice big windows facing south, into a school for our children and the Thorwaldsons. There was a class of eight. Jean was a wonderful teacher, and the children fell over one another to do things for her. Another great burden Jean took off my shoulders was the Sunday school, and it really prospered under her care. Some people are just born teachers, and Jean was one of them. We know she is still teaching today [1960] in a school in California, for we have kept in contact with her. She made such a tremendous contribution to our life in Little Grand Rapids.

The Indian Day School

Teaching the Indian day school after this was much easier, for naturally the progress of the native children was much slower. But we made good progress and it must have been lasting, for over twenty years later I received a letter from a teacher in Little Grand. He wanted to know what method I had used to teach, because none of the children were conversant in English except the ones I taught over twenty years ago. As a matter of fact, he said they were the

The chicken-house school: Gideon, Rhoda, and Betty (front); Shirley, Margaret, Bernice, Albert, Daniel, and Miss McConnell

The Indian day school: Luther Schuetze and his students

ones he was using for interpreters. Quite a feather in my cap.

I wrote back about the method, but don't know if it made any difference, for when we visited there in 1960, it was still the same. I believe the main reason was that they had so many teachers, none of them staying very long, not having had much love for either the place or the people. For love never fails, and children respond better when they are being loved.

A Surprise

During one of my absences, Ingeborg Thorwaldson enlisted the help of her husband and Alan Nelson, the Hudson's Bay clerk, so that when I returned and entered the church, I found that I had a pulpit for the first time. It was ingeniously constructed out of peeled birch and poplar poles about two inches in diameter, placed together perpendicular, resting on a board foundation and topped off with boards covered by a rich red velvet cloth. It really was a very pleasant surprise, and made me feel more at home holding services. It's certainly one of the rich experiences of life to be surprised by someone who cares.

Treating a Burn Victim

It was in the summer when one of our tests in the healing ministry came to us from Pauingassi, an eight-year-old girl. Her whole top torso was scalded with boiling fish soup knocked over from an airtight heater. They brought her to the point near the rapids. This had happened a day or so before, because I could detect the rotten odor of burned flesh even before I saw the little girl. It was a horrible sight and my heart sank. She had a high fever. All I could think about was Dr. Roy Bier's Healatone, which I had used before in minor burns, and which always somehow had a very soothing and pain-relieving influence.

This we used, and after a few days noticed a marked improvement. The little girl was well on the way to recovery when a nurse from Winnipeg came out with a little baby who had been sent in for an operation. I took her over and showed her the little girl's burns, which were now almost healed. The nurse threw up her hands and exclaimed, "It is a miracle, and a wonder that she lived!" So we had always so much to thank God for, and therefore, great encouragement in our work.

John Duck

However, the greatest miracle was yet to come, for modern man has accomplished many things in this age of science, but one thing he cannot do, and that is change the human heart. This is what happened to Machkojence, John Duck, the chief conjurer. The head medicine man's heart had been changed. On an unforgettable morning when I looked up on the hill, I saw two people coming down to the mission house, one with a great big bundle on his back. John always was a striking figure—tall, coal-black eyes that sometimes seemed to spew fire, and even now there was no stumbling or mumbling. He said: "I have come to give you this drum."

He had sold one like it not many years before to a Poplar Hill drummer for $500. Professor A. Irving

John Duck; courtesy of the Roman Catholic Church at Berens River with permission of the Oblates of Mary Immaculate in St. Boniface, Manitoba

Hallowell, of the University of Pennsylvania, sent out by the Smithsonian Institution, I believe, had tried to buy this one not long before, without success.[21] I was flabbergasted.

"It is evil," he said. "You can do with it whatever you like, smash it up or burn it. I will have no more to do with it. I and my wife, we want to be Christians."

I was deeply stirred, for I had been against this man's work right from the beginning. He had a good livelihood out of it, because everyone believed in his occult powers.

One Hudson's Bay clerk told me he had seen one of John Duck's demonstrations when Professor Hallowell asked him if he could find out, by conjuring, how his father was. So John built a conjuring tent right at the lakeshore, ramming down his stout poles so deep no one could shake them. Then he covered them with canvas and skins, and went inside to start his chant. The natives of Little Grand looked upon the turtle as one of man's greatest friends. It reaches a great age and is thought to be very wise. After a while the clerk said he heard a voice that sounded like it was coming from the water. I don't know whether this was lively imagination, but the turtle is often approached by the native conjurers. When John came out, apparently he said, "Your father has been very ill but is now on the mend, and there is a letter for you waiting in the post office at Berens River." This was about 108 miles downriver. And so it was!

No matter what I saw in John Duck, he was my greatest opponent in our work. He used to drum and chant in the evening, and everyone heard him. When a man had done something to displease John, he would make "medicine" against him. For instance, he would call in his musical invention that the person would not catch any furs that winter, and often it was so. If there had been a deadly insult, he would sing for the person's death, and often that person lay down and died, call it psychological effect or whatever you will. He was greatly feared, even by the white man, for most people have some kind of superstitious inclination.

I remember one day Bella Keeper and her mother came to me, both in tears, and said that John Duck had said Bella was going to die. Bella was a husky, fine-looking girl of about eighteen. I was mad and went to see John Duck right away. I told him that if he didn't stop this kind of stuff I would go to the police. I assured Bella and her mother that nothing was going to happen. It never did while I was there, but I heard later on that she was stabbed to death over in Ontario someplace.

Now here stood this man, not cringing or stuttering, but straight and erect. He had come to a decision to accept Jesus as his Saviour and Master.

"Well, John," I said, "I'll take this drum and write on it: This drum was given to me this date for the glory of God by John Duck," or something similar, "and keep it upstairs in our mission house, and if I go away, I will either destroy it or give it to some worthy person."

This I did. Later on when we intended to move, I gave it to Mr. Davidson, the credit manager of Ashdown's Wholesale, who was a Sunday school superintendent in a Winnipeg church. I asked him if he would put it in the museum in Winnipeg. And this he promised.

Medicines

The native people had a number of great medicines but no way of determining the exact dose to be taken. I will mention two instances. A plant that grows on almost all the rocky shores of the inland lakes is very effective in stopping the flow of menstrual blood. One woman kept on menstruating, so the medicine man brewed a potion of this plant and gave it to her. It was so strong that she, a comparatively young woman, never menstruated again and had no more children.

In another case, a young boy quite often had difficulty with urination, so his father, the son of a medicine man, always gave him a plant of the nightshade family, which relieved him right away. Then this man and his family moved over to the mainland where the soil was richer, with more clay than where he had lived before. Soon after, the boy had the same trouble. His father cooked him up the same potion and he was immediately relieved, but became stone blind. We believe that the richer soil gave the plant a greater potency. The poor boy never was able to see again.

Often instances and happenings like this drove the people more and more to our medicines and to us. I could get anything I wanted by requisition, but always had to send in five copies. We had remarkable success. Consequently we had more and more patients, even from the outlying districts, whose inhabitants always had to come through Little Grand Rapids on their way to the Berens River port. So we were busier and busier, loaded with more and more responsibility.

One day I was called over to the chief's, and here was the former Mary Boucher who had been with us on our trip to the Pacific coast. She was now Mrs. John Bear, the mother of two children.[22] She was lying in bed, quite sick and with severe pains on the right side of her abdomen. I looked and felt, but could feel nothing positive, for she had grown very fat with a thick layer on her abdomen. Finally I decided it was appendicitis, and made the decision to send her in by the first plane, which luckily came the next day. Then I wondered if I had made the right decision. Plane rides were expensive if they were chartered. I had paid $240 for my last charter.

We just had to wait and see. By this time we had radio connections and very good reception. We could depend on hearing Europe and Japan regularly. It was gratifying later on to know that we were right, and that Mary had gone just in time. When she returned home in perfect health, the worth of the white man's medicine went up a hundred per cent.

We ourselves enjoyed pretty good health with the exception of my occasional appendix attacks. When I drank a half cup of olive oil, the pain would subside. This hadn't happened for some time, and I hadn't laid in any fresh olive oil. One day an attack hit with excruciating pain. I looked for the olive oil, but there was only a cup left, and it was as rancid as could be. In desperation I downed it and became desperately ill, vomiting profusely. I thought I was going to die. This was almost thirty years ago, but I have never had another attack since.

Gusti and the children also had good health, with the exception of Rhoda. She'd had a nasty cough and poor appetite. We had her to the doctor in town, and Gusti took her to the doctor when the family lived in Winnipeg, but to no avail. I found that Scott's emulsion of cod liver oil helped her more than anything else. However, on one occasion she had a relapse and a worse attack of coughing. She hadn't slept for several nights because of the cough. Something occurred that I have never forgotten. Fritz was lying stretched out in the kitchen. Rhoda went in and laid her

Rhoda with Fritz

head on Fritz's flank, and the warmth and steady breathing somehow set her off to sleep. Poor Fritz became uncomfortable when this extended into hours. I can still see him lifting his head to see if he could get up, but he stayed there, I don't know for how long, until Rhoda finally woke up from a good, restful, coughless sleep. After that she was on the way with a steady improvement.

Sickness among our people became less and funerals scarcer. The people now had better housing and lived in ways more conducive to good health. They didn't dance anymore in their too-small houses, and drank less home brew.

Liquor Problems

This brings to mind one instance involving our good friend Maman Duck. There was some sort of public celebration. The RCMP were there and, apparently, Maman appeared to have been under the influence of liquor. He had a partly full bottle with him. He was arrested at once and taken down to Berens River for trial before Magistrate Disbrowe.

I arrived the day after and, as soon as I heard this, contacted Mr. Disbrowe, a former Hudson's Bay manager now retired. I begged him not to send Maman to jail, and said that if there was a fine we would go good for it. I explained to Mr. Disbrowe that if he took Maman away, the government would have to spend quite a sum for rations to feed some of the poor in Little Grand. Maman was perhaps the most successful hunter I ever knew, and the most open-hearted at giving. Whenever there appeared a shortage of food, Maman, as he told me, would dream, and the Good Spirit would tell him where the moose were. He would, invariably, take off the next morning and return sometimes the same day, most often the next, with a canoeload of meat to which everyone was welcome. He himself would take one or two pieces home. So Maman was fined, and we helped him to pay the fine.

Later on, Magistrate Disbrowe, who was a friend of mine,

told me he really was up a tree and didn't know what to do. "I have sent that bottle of liquor in to have it analyzed," he said, "and there was no percentage of alcohol in it whatsoever."

This was in confidence and never revealed until now. Maman may have had a drink or two somewhere else, or someone could have sold him this as liquor, which was not unusual. Some unscrupulous white men would go out in a canoe with a can of 65 o.p. alcohol together with several empty pop bottles, and as they trav-

Magistrate F.A. Disbrowe of Berens River [See Appendix C]

eled along, put a bit of the alcohol in a bottle and fill it with water from the lake or river, then later on, sell it for the same high price. Some bottles had no alcohol content at all. Whatever it was, we never found out, and Maman was exceedingly thankful and paid back the fine, for he was also a very successful trapper.

Trapping

I have seen Maman Duck and his brother Butchi Duck walk behind my sleigh coming home from Goose Lake, and it was already evening and sunset when they espied a fresh fisher track. The two never hesitated a moment, but without blankets or food took off after that fisher with the temperature away below zero. They would follow the track as long as they could see, and as soon as it was daylight, they'd take after the fisher again. A nice, small, female fisher would have been worth somewhere around $100, and that meant a lot of food and clothing for the children. Most often they succeeded in chasing the fisher up a tree or into a hole in the roots of a tree or stump. They would dig him out, kill and skin him, and go home rejoicing, trying to forget the gnawing hunger, the cold, and the sleepless night. One could not but help admire such men, and think of what possibilities lie dormant in these original Canadians so carelessly pushed aside, placed on reserves and forgotten.

Dealing with Health Problems

I once had the privilege to be of assistance to Maman Duck's wife. At the time they were living at Good Lake. Coming through there, I was told that while rubbing the clothes on the washboard, she had run a needle backward into the palm of her hand. I had a look at it but couldn't feel or see the broken needle in the hand. So on the way home, twenty-five miles away, I was worried and again thought the only source of help available is from our Lord. I found a pair of tweezers, filed them down to a very thin size, and then magnetized them on a heavy magnet that I had. I took this along with some bandages and disinfectant, made a little incision, and then probed for the needle piece. I was successful. I got hold of it and pulled it out. It was discoloured black. I cleansed the wound and put some thermofuge on a bandage, and it soon healed perfectly, thank the Lord.

It is strange that many occasions arise when you are far away from civilization, doctors, hospitals, or help of any kind, when you quickly turn to your Maker, as we often notice in disasters of any sort. People, when they look death in the face, always cry out to God for help. For example, we had the slogan during the war: "There are no atheists in foxholes," but in everyday life there seems to be no need for God. Yet if we would only realize how often little worries, like the little foxes that spoil the vines, chew away at our health. As the hymn writer Joseph M. Scriven so aptly puts it in one of our favourite hymns:

What a friend we have in Jesus,
All our sins and griefs to bear,
What a privilege to carry
Everything to God in prayer!
O what peace we often forfeit,
O what needless pain we bear,
All because we do not carry
Everything to God in prayer.

When you see so much need around you, and you have a
heart that cares and wants to render assistance, then it becomes
a habit, for you begin to realize how insignificant man really is
and how much he stands in need of Him who created this
incomprehensible universe.

There were more trials and more testing to come. A man
fell asleep with his candle burning in his mosquito bar in the
tent. The bar and bedding caught on fire, and the man's back
was badly burned. Dr. Roy's Healatone salve had become an
important factor in our household and again it came in good
stead, for the kind doctor supplied us with an abundance of
this salve, which had such pain-relieving and healing qualities.
This man, who was burned, belonged to the other mission,
but who cared when a man was in need? He made a good
recovery.

Then there was the little baby, about a year old, who had
a rupture near the navel. Gusti and I made a belt and encased
a button of the right dimension in some soft material, placed
it on the child, and it healed up completely. So many fractures
and cuts due to accidents.

There was one accident, though, I must mention for it, too,
was a miracle. I was playing outside at recess with the children.
We taught them many games. We left a few girls inside to do
certain duties in preparation for lunch, I think it was. There was
a shrill scream. I ran into the school and there stood a girl of
about ten or eleven with a piece of lead pencil sticking in the
iris of her eye. A smaller boy had sneaked in and was sharpen-
ing his pencil with a knife, like most boys do. It had a long piece
of lead on it that freed from the wood casing. The girl had tried

to chase him out, for he had no business there. He poked this pencil at her, and it went into the iris and broke off.

I was horrified, and in my haste did the wrong thing. I pulled it out and immediately the eye jelly, I forget the technical name for it, came out. I quickly pulled the eyelid down and put my finger over it, praying all the time. I rushed her outside and kept putting snow on it. I don't know what made me do it but, apparently, it was the right thing to do. I took her home and bandaged up the eye, putting on some eye lotion. Well, I prayed more earnestly for a plane. None came, since it was a bad time of the year. I took the girl into a dark room and renewed the bandage every day.

After two weeks a plane came. I took the girl into the dark room, took the bandage off, and let a bit of light in.

Miss McConnell and her Sunday School class

"Can you see?"

"Yes."

I opened the blind fully. She could see perfectly, but had a little scar in the iris right below the pupil. The scar was clearly visible, yet the girl could see even when I closed the other eye.

It was a time of humble thanksgiving to the ever-present Lord, invisible to the physical eye but not to the eye of faith, always the same yesterday, today, and forever, in His wonderful compassionate divine love. When later on in the summer I mentioned this to the inspector of Indian agencies in Winnipeg, he said that they had had a similar case of a boy with an eye punctured by a lead pencil. He was operated on and had lost his sight.

15

MUSIC IN THE AIR

1938

The Good Times

Some people have the idea that when you are away from our so-called civilization you are leading a sacrificial life. Nothing could be further from the truth! Now when we look back, we can verify what we then suspected—that we were living a fuller, happier life than we lived before, or have since. There was no dullness whatsoever.

First there was the beauty of nature ever with us in its changing moods, in the different seasons and the different times of day. The early sunrise decked the trees with an extra beauty. Sometimes as many as forty wild grouse picked away on the tops of the silvery maple trees, and in the evening a like number of partridges took their place—birds of every kind. We used to send in reports on the birds to the Winnipeg Tribune, in "Chickadee Notes." On a summer's evening, looking out of our mission house window, we saw the moon shining on the lake's wavelets around evergreen-crowned islands. These moments are forever engraved upon our memories.

Pets and Wild Creatures

Then we had pets: of course Fritz, more or less a member of the family; a canary named Pat, given to me in Portland and what a beautiful singer; and a cat who was very understanding. One time we had run out of meat. I was going fall fishing, and promised Gusti that I'd come back the next day with a catch. Upon returning with the promised fish, I was told that the cat, on the same afternoon I had left, went out hunting and brought home, right into the kitchen, a ruffed grouse that she had killed.

Then there was the porcupine I had picked up while haying, and put in a fenced, board-bottom enclosure. Here I saw for the first time that the porcupine throws quills with its tail when angered, and these quills will stick right into board. I freed the porky later on, but it wouldn't leave us until I took it farther away.

Little Grand Rapids

There was also a young fox vixen that I brought home for a pet. I had set some traps and snares while fall fishing, and sometimes brought home a goodly number of pelts. This one was young and alive and not hurt. We kept her for quite awhile, then finally let her go. I'm certain it was she that later on mated and had a litter of pups close by.

Now I will tell about the bear cub. He frightened Gusti several times as he grew bigger and would come into the kitchen for the fish. When she tried to put him out, he'd grab her around the legs and she'd scream to me for help. I had to get rid of him the next spring, so I took him to Matheson Island and gave him away. They finally took him across the channel to the main shore, which was a game reserve. There he came to a bad end. A traveller had pulled his skiff ashore and was boiling the kettle, as the saying goes, when our bear, now almost fully grown, saw him and came to visit. The traveller panicked, grabbed his rifle, and shot him.

I have learned since that it doesn't pay to pamper the wild creatures, for then they look upon all men as bene-factors and fall easy prey to unscrupulous people, having lost that suspicious, wild instinct that keeps them alert and alive. This was all too evident with one of the greatest pets we had up there, a horned owl we called Squeaky. We raised her from a little downy thing into a magnificent bird of great plumage and beauty. When she got big enough (she was still downy) we let her out. When she wanted to come in or was hungry, she'd come to the kitchen window and would knock at the windowpane by pecking at it, at the same time making a little squeaky noise. She was a wonderful pet and would come at the slightest call. Even if she sat in the highest tree she would come right to me at once, without much coaxing. We finally left her outside altogether, and sometimes she would disappear for a little while, but always came back each day.

When we finally had to leave Little Grand, we ordered a plane to take us down. On the day of our departure, I called Squeaky and took her into the kitchen, for I thought she might be away when the plane came. But the plane didn't arrive as expected and it was turning toward evening, so I felt sorry for our pet and let her out. She gratefully winged her way over the tall spruce and disappeared. Just then the plane landed. We boarded with all our goats and dogs and cat, and I left word to send our pet owl down with the next plane the following day.

When the plane came, Squeaky was there. They called her, and she came down and sat on the ground before them. Then a big dog, their pet, pounced and killed her. Never again did I harbour or tame any wild animal or bird.

Fishing Stories

There were amusing incidents too, such as when Gusti, Mrs. Thorwaldson, and I, late in the spring, took our 17-foot canoe and pulled along on the candled ice. We knew the fish were running at Root Creek Portage, about four miles away, and there were several dogs to feed. I continually cautioned the women to hang on tight to the canoe in case we broke through. We were rounding a point, almost there, when the ice gave way. First one woman and then the other

Sucker Rapids: Herman at left; Miss Mosel in white

went down, and while I was telling them to hang on tight, I myself went down. Luckily it wasn't too deep; we were in just over our waist. Despite the cold water, we had to laugh at one another.

After we had extricated ourselves, we got to the open water without further mishap, and up to the Little Falls. There were fish in abundance, and we soon filled all our containers. It is quite a thing to catch a 3- or 4-pound fish (these were suckers) and then hang onto him.

This story makes me think of Miss Mosel, whom we once had out on such an expedition. She got one nice fish and held him in both hands right in the middle, but instead of throwing him ashore, she started to walk out with the wiggling fish slipping farther and farther through her hands. As Miss Mosel screamed at all this wiggling, the fish got free and flopped back into the water.

One of the most colourful fish at Little Grand was the pickerel, Gusti's favourite eating fish. Their run was from Ugans Saminichgamen, a swift current place, to a small lake some miles south of Little Grand. There you could see them easily—beautiful, shining, ever-changing green. They were easily caught and made ready to cook. No scaling to do, just a few strokes with a sharp knife, and there lay the loveliest fillets you ever saw, ready for the frying pan.

And still, amongst nature's abundant supply there were times when the fish seemed to disappear. This happened especially in the summertime when the water became warmer. So there were some people who went hungry, mostly, though, because they had become accustomed to the white man's ways of sundry supplies that came from the production line and cost money, something most didn't have. As a matter of fact, we hardly ever saw or handled money in our eleven years at Little Grand.

Of course, we had ample resources in the bank and good credit. We could get anything we wanted, and after a while write out a cheque. But practically the only time the natives saw money was at treaty time, and they got rid of it as soon as possible. Honest people had good credit at the trading posts, but if it wasn't good, often hardships were involved. As a rule, the native inland people were the most natural communists I have ever seen, always sharing with one another.

Helping a Roman Catholic

I remember one time in the winter, we were asked to come see Papaski at the very end of the reserve. He was a pagan, but belonged to the R.C. Mission, which was right near his house. When I got there it was not so serious at all. The old fellow had been out trapping and twisted his ankle; it was quite swollen and hot. I asked him, "Why did you not get the priest who lives right here, and to whose church all your family belongs?"

"I did," he said, "but he just made it worse. I did not sleep all night, and the pain seemed to be getting worse."

I immersed his foot in hot water, and sent over some liniment, but I had to go again to make sure everything was all right.

Challenging Questions

This brings me to a quaint request by old Pandakik. It was after the Sunday forenoon service. He was an old man, not so spry anymore and the last one out. He warmly shook my hands and said, "You said the great God created the earth and all that is in it."

"Yes," I replied, "that is right."

"Well," he continued, "did God create man to be hungry?"

"No," I told him.

"Well, I have had nothing to eat since yesterday."

So of course, I had to take him home and give him something to eat.

Now talk about children asking embarrassing questions. One day while many others stood around, a child said, "You have read to us out of the Kitche Masinaigan (The Great Book) that Cain took himself a wife. Where did he find a wife when the great Book teaches us that God only created two people, Adam and Eve?"

I answered, "You must have noticed that I said people reached a great old age in the beginning of time, and that Adam and Eve had many more children, some of whom wandered far. Cain must have come upon one of his sisters and married her. You know that still happens even among you people today." So that's how I got out of that one.

But another time on a 160-mile road trip, while Wawak and I were boiling the kettle, which means having something to eat along the road (it was very good, as its warmth saturated us), a whisky-jack, properly known as Canada jay, lit upon a branch nearby. Looking up, Wawak said, apropos of nothing, "Why did God create the whisky-jack?"

Now I knew the natives hated the whisky-jack, for this bird is an inquisitive fellow and often follows a trapper around while he builds his deadfalls or sets his traps, knowing there is usually something to be had to eat. When the man is gone, the whisky-jack hops down and inspects things. Often there is some bait of fish, meat, or fowl stuck on a little stick back of the trap to lure the fur-bearing animal. Well, the whisky-jack hops in and steals that bait, thus taking away the attraction. Sometimes he gets caught in the trap and loses his life.

Whichever happens, a week or two later the trapper comes along. He sees fresh fisher tracks going in the right direction toward his set. His step quickens and his heart beats faster as he visualizes all the food and new clothing he will be able to buy, which his family so badly needs. He comes to his set—the bait has been stolen. The fisher, whose pelt would have been worth around one hundred dollars if it was a small, dark female, passed right in front of his set. He is mad, for he sees by the signs who spoiled his hope, and he swears vengeance on the whisky-jack. So when Wawak asked me why God created the whisky-jack, I knew what was in his mind.

I thought quickly and said, "You no doubt have heard that several moose have been found dead recently, skinny and full of wood ticks. The reason is that you people have killed so many whisky-jacks and he's the one who has to do the job of picking off the wood ticks. You must have seen him doing it!"

"Yes, I have," Wawak answered. And as soon as he said that, the thought came to me: O my gosh, what will I tell him if he asks why God created the wood tick? I was glad he didn't.

A Wedding to Remember

Perhaps the most embarrassing moment that ever happened was at the wedding of a young white couple in our new church. I asked the usual question: "Therefore, if any man can show any just cause why they may not lawfully be joined together, let him now speak or else hereafter forever hold his peace."

A young native woman stood up. The church was full, because a wedding was a great occasion for festivity. "I protest," she said, "because he was going to marry me, and I am bearing his child."

So the wedding was off for that day! I called the young woman in with the couple and confronted her. She steadfastly proclaimed the same thing. The man, who had been through the district many times, shamefully admitted that he had had relations with her, but that he had never promised to marry her. This must have been very trying to the young bride, and I expected her to walk out and say good-bye forever to the groom-to-be. The native woman continued to stress the fact that she had no income, and that the man should have to share the burden of bringing the baby into the world.

Finally the bride spoke up, for we were getting no place. "Elizabeth," she said, "I will be glad to take your baby as my very own when it is born."

We all were thunderstruck, and it took the wind out of Elizabeth's sails. She left soon after, saying that she would no longer interfere in the wedding, and kept her word when the marriage was completed.

An Organ for the Church

We missed having an organ in the church and felt the need of it. I didn't want to take the other one out of the school where I used it every morning in our short devotional period. So I finally ordered one, but didn't hear of its arrival at Matheson Island where we had asked that it be sent. Finally word came that it had arrived and now was at George Leyound's at Bloodvein. I talked it over with one of the pilots of Wings Limited, I believe it was, and he said they had a plane big enough to bring it up. One Sunday afternoon he landed on his way back to Winnipeg, saying he'd have time to get it, so I went with him to Bloodvein.

The organ was there all right, but much too tall to go through the door. I borrowed a saw and cut the top off, but the organ was also too long. The pilot decided to leave the door open with about two feet of organ sticking out. It didn't take long to make Little Grand, but it was the closest I came to freezing to death, for I hadn't changed my Sunday clothing and sat next to the open door. With the speed of the plane and the temperature about thirty below zero—was I

Luther Schuetze and the congregation outside the church, 1938

ever glad when we landed! Even after unloading, I couldn't write my signature on the cheque in the usual manner. I had to hold the pen with my whole hand. We fastened on the sawed-off top perfectly. No one knew it had been cut off unless it was examined closely.

Later on we found a big headline in all the papers in Winnipeg: "Music in the Air." It really was quite a feat for the pilot, since the space on the Bloodvein River was limited, especially with the organ sticking out. When the press found out about this, they played it up in their usual manner.

Now we had an organ in our church and a perfect organist in Jean McConnell. Jean was also a great help in conducting our Sunday school. She had such a winning personality that the children waited for Sunday with anticipation, and our Sunday school attendance was almost one hundred percent.

Social Life

Life at the mission had taken on a newer aspect of sociability, with the Thorwaldson family being so close, with Jean, and with the Hudson's Bay personnel. I was glad for Gusti's sake. For all these years she had been very, very busy with the little ones, but had no one to talk to, since she couldn't master the native language. There were evenings of games and crossword puzzles, and outside there was horseshoe pitching.

One evening our wives chided us for no longer being romantic, otherwise we would take them out on a moonlight canoe ride. It was one of those lovely, clear nights under full moon, with silvery streams of light shimmering across the gently moving waves. We called their bluff, and pretty soon you could see canoes with couples slowly drifting and paddling along.

I wonder if it was an evening like this that changed Jean's life, for she later married Alan Nelson, then the Hudson's Bay clerk. The Nelsons now reside in California with their almost-grown family, Jean still teaching school. The

Playing horseshoes at the mission: Mr. Leslie, H.B.Co. Post manager, left

Thorwaldsons also live in that state [1960]. It is really too bad that Canada is losing so much of its pioneer stock, but no matter where they are, they will be worthy representatives and workers for good.

And so we were on the march in Little Grand, with conditions improving in every way. The general health was improving; TB was on the wane. We were a cleaner, brighter settlement with bigger and better houses now under the Christian influence. Already you could see a vast difference from the tiny settlement of Pauingassi, just ten miles away.

I have often thought if more of our people, in particular the women, could see the difference, and realize how much they owe to the influence of the church upon their lives, they would be more thankful for our Christian faith. They would thank God every day, and give themselves more unreservedly and enthusiastically for the cause of Christ.

Agriculture at Little Grand Rapids

Gardens were springing up here and there. I still remember Sasho Keeper coming over with a huge cucumber he had grown, wondering what he should do with it. However, in my estimation, Little Grand Rapids will never lend itself to a livelihood from agriculture. It is mainly of granite rock formation, and unless industry can be developed, there isn't much of a future for the people. I pointed this out to them, and quite a number were interested in asking the Department to relocate them to the mouth of the Pigeon River, at Lake Winnipeg. It has a much more fertile appearance, with fairly large hayfields and less rock. Transportation would be easy, for the Pigeon River, like the Berens River, flows out of Family Lake, only in a southerly direction.

This idea, however, was soon squashed by the old people. They said: You remember how so-and-so moved to Berens River and other places at the lake? They are all dead now, and if we move down there, we will soon be all gone and none of us would be left.

So that was it. Perhaps it's just as well. However, they'll have to partly migrate again and again, for there won't be enough room for them all in Little Grand.

Farewell

Little Grand Rapids is a beautiful place, and memories of its sounds still tug at our hearts. Like a grand orchestra, they make melodies that speak of the Almighty Creator. The deep roar of the falls serves as background to leaves rustling, birds singing, and wavelets gently lapping on rocky and sandy shores.

Soon we were to feel the sweet sorrow of parting from the place we had hewn out of the wilderness; from the warmth and the comfort of the home that we had built with our own hands, and in which we found love and sorrow for nearly eleven years; from the gentle earth that held the bodies of our beloved. For we had been transferred to Berens River.

The Rev. Mr. Niddrie had laboured there for nineteen years and had asked the Presbytery if I might be his successor. This was a great compliment, for Mr. Niddrie was a great and at the same time humble soul, fully dedicated to our Lord and His task of labouring among the natives.

Augusta and Luther just before leaving Little Grand Rapids, 1938

Epilogue

This has been the story of Luther Schuetze, a man who took his family up the Berens River in a canoe in 1927, and then he brought them down eleven years later by airplane. He went up to Little Grand Rapids as a trader hired to teach and preach for the new United Church of Canada. But before long he was a dentist, doctor, and Indian Agent as well. From logs, he built a church and a house, a barn for horses and goats, as well as storage sheds. He repaired outboard motors and hauled supplies with his horses in the winter. He dispensed medicine for the sick, food rations for the needy, and used clothes sent by church women in the East. All these things were done in addition to preaching and teaching, marrying and burying. It is therefore easy to understand why the people coming to see him asked for Kiss-che Ogema, which means headman or boss.

In 1938 Luther succeeded the Reverend John Niddrie as minister to the church in Berens River, Manitoba. Then in 1942 Luther moved his family to Goble, and then to Rainier, Oregon. He worked in the sawmill at Prescott, and was associate minister at the Methodist Church in Rainier. In 1945 he returned to British Columbia as lay missionary to the people at Bella Coola. He served the local community church, the Lutheran Church at Hagensborg, as well as the Immanuel Indian Church. He brought these two other churches into the United Church of Canada.

Luther was ordained by the B.C. Conference of the United Church on May 13, 1949, while serving in Bella Coola. One of his fellow ordinands was Peter Kelly, the Haida Chief and lay preacher who served many years on various charges, including the Thomas Crosby, a United Church motor launch that travelled the coast serving logging and fishing camps.

The Reverend Schuetze was transferred to the Keremeos–Hedley–Cawston charge in 1953. This three-point territory also included the community at the Nickel

Plate Mine, which he visited regularly. He later served as assistant minister in the Penticton United Church from 1961 to 1965.

Luther lived in retirement at Penticton until his death on December 20, 1979. His body was buried in the Penticton cemetery. He is survived by his wife Augusta (who continues to live in Penticton) and sons, daughters, and their children.

Return to Little Grand Rapids and the Beginnings of this Book

When Luther returned to Little Grand Rapids for a visit in 1960 as the Reverend Schuetze, he was greeted by old friends. He had worked for their benefit in the old days; now they came to share in worship together, one last time, before he left them for good. Luther's old friend Tom Boulanger went up the Berens River with canoes to bring him back down the rapids and portages that he had known so well. This was to refresh his memory for the book he planned to write. Luther finished the book in 1964, but it did not get published. Tom Boulanger's book, An Indian Remembers, came out in 1971. In 1987 Luther's widow, Augusta Schuetze, presented a copy of his memoir to the United Church of Canada Archives located at the University of Winnipeg. In 1997 a family document including this memoir (somewhat edited by his son Ernest, and with additional pictures) was circulated to family members. A copy was also left at the same United Church Archives.

These then are the forerunners of the book we put before you in the year 2001. Since the year 2000 was the year of the United Church of Canada's 75th Anniversary, it seems like a good time to bring out Luther's memoir as a look back to the Church's very beginnings. Perhaps we can get some sense of how far we have come as a part of the Body of Christ in those 75 years.

The United Church no longer sends out missionaries within Canada, or even to distant lands. It may send persons abroad if a request is made from its partner Church in that country. It is just as likely to invite a person from other lands to come and serve in our churches here, for we can learn from those vital newer Christians.

In 1974, the United Church joined with other national churches in an ecumenical effort called Project North. This was to support First Nations in the Berger Inquiry into the proposed MacKenzie River pipeline project. This was also to assist the churches in developing policy and response to justice issues such as resource development. In 1989 Project North was restructured as the Aboriginal Rights Coalition (ARC), a new partnership between national churches and church bodies, First Nations and local network groups across the country.

In the meantime, The United Church of Canada had apologized to Native Congregations in 1986, and the national churches had released A New Covenant recognizing the rights of Aboriginal Peoples to be distinct peoples, to adequate land bases, and to self-determination in 1987. The United Church's Apology to Native Congregations reads as follows:

> Long before my people journeyed to this land your people were here, and you received from your elders an understanding of creation, and of the Mystery that surrounds us all that was deep and rich and to be treasured.

> We did not hear you when you shared your vision. In our zeal to tell you of the good news of Jesus Christ we were blind to the value of your spirituality.

> We confused Western ways and culture with the depth and length and height of the gospel of Christ.

> We imposed our civilization as a condition for accepting the gospel.

We tried to make you like us and in doing so we helped to destroy the vision that made you what you were. As a result you and we are poorer and the image of the Creator in us is twisted, blurred, and we are not what we were meant by the Great Spirit to be.

We who represent the United Church of Canada ask you to forgive us and to walk together in the spirit of Christ so that our people may be blessed and God's creation healed."

(General Council, August 15, 1986, Sudbury, Ontario)

First Nation Elders have received, but not accepted, this apology. If the conviction to walk together in the spirit of Christ is achieved, there will cease to be racism and prejudice against the original people of this land.

Herman L. Schuetze
November 2000

Appendix A

The Hudson's Bay Company Presence at Little Grand Rapids
(from Hudsons Bay Company Archives)

Chartered in **1670**, the Hudson's Bay Company established posts on the shores of James Bay as well as Hudson Bay. It established the English presence there, flying the Red Ensign with the initials HBC on the fly. The French ruled Canada, and the English exerted influence through the Company.

After **1763**, the Montreal traders replaced the French traders on the lakes and rivers. The English now ruled Canada. The Company also set up posts and sent men into the interior to compete with these "free" traders.

In **1801**, David Sanderson established the first Hudson's Bay Company post at what he called Big Fall, later to be known as Little Grand Rapids. He built a house and traded for furs. In the spring, he headed back to Osnaburgh House on the Albany River, upstream from Albany Fort on James Bay. The next fall, he returned to Big Fall House with supplies, and he continued this pattern of travel for four years.

In **1816**, Donald Sutherland came from York Factory to build a house, fortified with a stockade, for the Hudson's Bay Company. He named the place Great Falls House, and it became the centre of the company's trade east of Lake Winnipeg. York boats were rowed and sailed on the waterways, bringing furs to York Factory and supplies to the posts. In **1821**, the two companies merged, and when George Simpson restructured the new Hudson's Bay Company, he abandoned Great Falls House.

In **1848**, William McKay, manager of the Hudson's Bay Company post at Berens River, established an outpost at Great Falls House, now known as Grand Rapids of the Berens River.

In **1865** William Isbister wintered at Grand Rapids to collect furs, then from 1866 to 1871, William McKay resided there.

During these years, there were considerable changes. Canadian Confederation occurred in **1867**. Then, in **1869**, Canada acquired the Hudson's Bay Company lands and took responsibility for governing them. Following fast was the formation of a new province: Manitoba entered Confederation in **1870**.

From that time until **1932**, the Hudson's Bay post at Grand Rapids on the Berens River had two John Moars. The first John Moar was born in the Orkney Islands in **1843**. He joined the company in **1861**, and was with the Berens River people when they "took treaty" in **1875**. He also witnessed the inclusion of Grand Rapids into the enlarged province of Manitoba in **1888**. And when his son succeeded him as manager in **1912**, Manitoba had reached the size it is today. John adapted well to his life in the New World, learning the Anishinabe language and working his way up in the company that he served so diligently.

John Moar Jr. was born in Sandy Lake in **1869**. He grew up with the language of his native mother and in the company life of his father. He succeeded his father at the Little Grand Rapids post, and over the years saw the disappearance of the York boats on Lake Winnipeg and the coming of the steamboats. Men went back to freighting with canoes, then outboard motors appeared, making life easier. Soon airplanes were being used in the Forest Service. Life was changing in his world. Johnnie Moar died in Selkirk, Manitoba, as his father had before him. His descendants continue to live at Little Grand Rapids.

In **1941**, the Hudson's Bay Company post was destroyed by fire and rebuilt in a new location, next to the graveyard belonging to the United Church. Luther Schuetze found it there when he visited Little Grand Rapids in **1960**. Since then, the Hudson's Bay Company has given up its trading posts and is now only involved in large city stores. The company's store at Little Grand Rapids has become a Northern store.

Appendix B

Richard Remembers

Following are excerpts from an audiotape memoir by Richard Schuetze, recorded on October 21, 1978, at the residence of Herman Schuetze in Surrey, B.C.

Richard Oswald Schuetze was born in Manitoba, Canada, on June 15, 1913. However, the taped memoir did not include the reason why Richard came to the Luther Schuetze family in 1927, nor anything about his life prior to this arrival.

Herman Schuetze: Richard traveled by train to Winnipeg, where he caught the S. S. Wolverine on its voyage north on Lake Winnipeg's East Coast. He disembarked at the Georges Island stop. From there he traveled by boat, with at least one other person, to some intermediate place, probably Poplar Point. Father picked him up in his "gas boat" and took him to the Schuetze Trading Post. The gas boat had been a sailing boat that was converted to one powered by a Chevrolet engine, for the purpose of carrying goods for the trading post from Georges Island.

Richard says that the trip to Little Grand Rapids started with the voyage to Berens River on that same gas boat later christened the Ivory.

From Berens River the trip was by canoe up that same river to Little Grand Rapids. He remembers the dogs Dick and Trap being up at Little Grand Rapids, but isn't sure whether they went up on that trip.

Richard arrived at Poplar River about the middle of July 1927, and believes that the trip to Little Grand Rapids was made in August of that year. He remembers "the school there, and this other building. It was a log cabin right close by. It wasn't very big, about like the Indian houses. Later there was a lean-to added."

He was there "about from August when we came, until after Christmas of that same year. That was 1927." Then "we went down to Berens River...we went direct from Little Grand Rapids to Berens, with the dogs Dick and Trap. I was the runner...running ahead of the dogs on snowshoes ...and I know I had some problems. I had never been on a trail, you know. I was new to all that sort of thing.

"We got there December 31st, and Dad had injured his ankle. I don't know, sprained it or what. And he was looking forward to being able to soak it in hot water, but no such luck. Mr. Niddrie, who was the missionary at Berens River at that time, asked him if he wouldn't mind speaking at the Watchnight Service. Which he did. And of course he didn't get a chance to soak his foot as soon as he would have liked.

"I stayed with the Streets. He was the schoolteacher there. He lived right across the Berens River, upstream a little ways. About a quarter of a mile.

"So I went to school with Mr. Street, took my Grade 8 there. And in the summer I went back to Little Grand Rapids with Dad. He came down to get me.

"Well, I spent all that summer, which would be the summer of 1928, at Little Grand Rapids. And then in the fall he took me down. We went to Winnipeg. I think we went down by boat from Berens River to Winnipeg. I stayed with the Steins there, out on Pacific Avenue toward the West Side of downtown Winnipeg there. And I went to Wesley College there. That was Grade 9. And then to the end of the year, which would be the summer of 1929. Then that summer I went back to Little Grand Rapids. Then back down in the fall again to school in Winnipeg. That was Grade 10. Then at the end of that school year I went back to Little Grand Rapids. And then back to Winnipeg to take my Grade 11. Then back to Little Grand Rapids.

"I went back to Little Grand Rapids and stayed there for the summer. That would be 1931. I stayed there until Jimmy Kirkness died, then I went up there to finish out the year. I think that was 1934.

"Rolfie died that fall of 1931. Then we took the trip to the United States in the summer of 1932. I'm sure it was Grandpa who stayed and looked after the place while we were gone.

"We went to Winnipeg by canoe. Then we drove to the West Coast to visit relatives. After we returned to Winnipeg we got in our canoe and headed up Lake Winnipeg again.

"When the wind was with us we put up a sail, and sailed with the wind. The motor that we had was the 'bannock-maker'...quay-she-gun ah-poo...or flour soup...that's what the Indian word means, flour-juice or flour soup. Quayshegunahpoo, that was the Anishinabe name. Dad called it the 'bannock-maker.'

"...and the canoe, the turtle...Misqua-tay see or something like that. He had widened it at the back so that it looked just like the shell of a turtle, you know. Yes, that was the most stable canoe.

"I don't remember when it was that Jimmy Kirkness died. He was a missionary at Pikangikum, and he died. I don't know where he came from. I think he came from Norway House or from up that way. Anyway he was Cree, that is, part Cree, and he went as a missionary to the Pikangikum people. I don't know how long he was there. He was a nice old person.

"So when he died I went up there and stayed the rest of that year. Then at least one more year, you know, the following year. William Keeper went up with me then. He was from Little Grand Rapids.

"I was there, like I say, at least that year and another full year.

It might have been two more years. I'm not sure. Anyway, then I went back to Wesley College taking first-year Arts and Sciences.

"It's no longer Wesley College. The name has changed to United Colleges. It was Wesley College and this other one a few blocks away. One was called Manitoba College. They united. That's why it was called United Colleges. This Manitoba College is not to be confused with the University of Manitoba. Those are two different entities. Yes there was a separate university, and that is where I wrote my exams, at the University. Then I went back to Little Grand Rapids.

"It was one of those years...I can't remember when it was, that I stayed up at Little Grand Rapids for the winter. That was the winter that we freighted with the horses, you know. With the hackneys, Bob and Princess. I drove the buckskins, Dobbin and Molly. We made six trips that winter, as a matter of fact, freighting supplies.

"I don't know how the supplies got to Bloodvein, perhaps on the ice from Fisher River, with other teams.

"We made one trip in only five days. That's the round trip. Six days, one trip was seven days, and two trips eight days, I think. A total of six trips, the maximum was eight days. The fastest one was five days. They had three camps there. The first camp when you're going from Little Grand Rapids was at Goose Lake. The halfway camp, roughly half way, was Mud Lake. The third camp closest to Bloodvein was at a lake called Long-body Lake. That was the translation of the Indian name for it. We had cabins at each of those lakes.

"Dad built the camps. Other people may have used that route, but he built the camps. I'm pretty sure that he did... at least the ones at Goose Lake and Mud Lake. I don't know about the one at Long-body Lake, because it is pretty hard to get into in the summer...maybe from Bloodvein, I don't know.

"We had quite an experience on one of those trips, coming back to Little Grand Rapids. You know how in some winters it freezes up and the ice gets real thick, and there's still not much snow. That's good, but you have something called glare ice to contend with. Some winters it would snow fairly heavily just after freeze-up. When it did that, the ice wouldn't get as thick as it did in the winters there was no snow on the ice.

"This one time there was a lot of snow on the ice. With the weight of it, I guess, the water would seep up and, you know, form slush, and you couldn't see it at all. Coming from Mud Lake we got into some of that as we came into Goose Lake. One of those trips we got into that, and it was evening, and all this slush. It really slowed us down. We got our feet wet. Of course it froze on our moccasins, a coating of ice, you know.

"Well, we had to unload the sleighs, carry the stuff past the slush, and then drive the horses. That time, I'm pretty sure...wait a minute...let's see now. That time we only had one team of horses on that trip we made. Just the one team and Dad drove. He almost froze his feet...his toes, you know. Because when the sleigh was reloaded he had to ride while driving the horses. You know, when you drive a team in the bush you can't walk beside the sleigh and drive the team. There's no room for that. He had to sit on the sleigh. But I was walking behind, so I wasn't in the plight that he was...you see.

"Well, when we got into Goose Lake Camp, it was past midnight, a way past midnight. We got a red fire going. We got that tin heater red-hot. Then we put our moccasined feet right up against that heater. They were cased in ice, you know, from walking through that slush. We thawed them out, and I guess that it was at least three o'clock in the morning, you know, before we turned in. That was really an experience. I guess Dad did really freeze his toes. They used to say that when you froze your face, you know, you rub it with snow. Course he couldn't do that, when he got his feet wet. That was quite an experience!"

Herman: About what he was hauling, Richard mentioned provisions, and was unsure about building materials. He was pretty sure that if there were any they would be for the church, as the house was already built.

Richard: "I guess it would have to be, because we wouldn't have had to make all those trips for just provisions, you know. I know we were living in the house at the time and still going to church, you know, on the reserve.

"But at breakup time it's pretty hard to get over. There's a time there that it's pretty hard to get across. It's quite impossible, as the lakes are impassible. There's not enough open water for a canoe, and of course, the ice is too weak to walk on.

"At freeze-up it's the same thing. We have a time when we just have to wait…can't go by canoe and can't walk.

"I finally left the family in 1939. In the fall we went down. I guess that we must have gone down by S.S. Keenora to Winnipeg, south, that is. It was September. The war had just begun. We were surprised that I could get across the border, you know, being of military age. Yeah, it was September, 1939.

"From there we went by Greyhound bus to Seattle. That's where we ended up. I don't remember whether we changed buses or not. Anyway, we went through the Crow's Nest Pass. We went by Blairmore, Fernie, and Cranbrook. We crossed into Idaho, Sandpoint, Bonner's Ferry, Spokane and west to Seattle. That was 1939."

Appendix C

Excerpts from Brother Leach's Story: 1926 to 1927

Brother Frederick Leach spent one year teaching at the Roman Catholic Mission at Little Grand Rapids. Born in London, England, in 1892, Frederick Leach emigrated to Canada at the age of nineteen. After working as a farm labourer, he turned to teaching and, in 1913, joined the Oblates at Lachine, Quebec. In 1920, Brother Leach pronounced his Perpetual Vows as Oblate of Mary Immaculate at Berens River, Manitoba. For many years Brother Leach's missionary work involved educating the children in the areas where he was stationed, which included Berens River, Bloodvein River, and Little Grand Rapids. He retired in St. Boniface, Manitoba, in 1978, and passed away on July 12, 1982, at the age of 90. Following are excerpts from his memoirs, 60 Years with Indians and Settlers on Lake Winnipeg, revised for clarity with the permission of the Oblates of Mary Immaculate in St. Boniface, Manitoba.[23]

Canoe Trip to Little Grand Rapids

There are approximately forty-six falls and rapids between Berens and Little Grand Rapids, necessitating portaging through bush paths or over rocky ridges, and, as at that time there were no outboard engines, one had to paddle all the way, so getting our freight up to Little Grand Rapids was no small feat.

Referring back to my diary, I am able to give you some idea as to what one of these trips was like at that time.

Three trips had already been made, but I had to come back to Berens to get the rest of our equipment.

This last trip was started on October 21, quite late in the season for freighting. On the first day the two guides and I made only five portages. We had started out a little late in the day, and it was rather slow work, as extra care had to be taken, due to the rain and sleet showers which had fallen a few days previous to our start, making the bush and rocks slippery. About six miles from the mouth of the river is a rapid where years ago an Englishman was drowned, hence its name, "Englishman's Rapids." During the next three days we made twenty-nine portages, one of them at Conjuring Falls. In bygone days the Indian "medicine men" liked this spot on the river to beat their drums and perform various rites.

As time passed, we began to get a little worried. On some of the small river bays a skim of ice was forming. At Flag Portage we had to break some with our paddles. This spot on the river is so named from the fact that the first Indian Agent, Mr. Angus McKay, camped there on the day that Queen Victoria was celebrating her Diamond Jubliee. In honour of the event, Mr. McKay gave his men a holiday and hoisted a Union Jack up a tree trimmed for the purpose. His men went for a hunt, killed a moose, and thus provided themselves with several good meals. Not too far from Flag Portage is Old Fort Rapids, where in 1816, the Hudson's Bay Company had an outpost for a short time. We also passed the Queen's Chair. From a short distance away this rock formation really looks like a huge chair. The base is formed by a huge square rock and the back by a high thin slab almost touching the base.

On October 25 we faced a headwind. My two guides were used to paddling and didn't seem too tired, but my arms certainly ached, so I was very glad when we made it rather a short day. We decided to camp just above Moose Painted Falls, so named because many, many years ago an Indian painted a picture of a moose on a fairly huge rock. The red colouring used must certainly have been of excellent quality, as the outlines were still visible in spite of such a long exposure to the weather. When passing it, many an Indian used to throw a piece of tobacco in the river. This was supposed to bring good luck.

Our last day of travel was the easiest. Most of it was done through a number of lakes. We had only one long portage to make, and this was at Night Owl Falls. Little Grand Rapids was reached in the afternoon of the sixth day. The same trip today could be made by airplane in forty minutes.

The first white man ever to come down the full length of the Berens River was William Tomison, in 1767. He made his way up the Severn River from the Hudson Bay, and crossed over to the headwaters of the Berens River, which he descended to its outlet in Lake Winnipeg.

No Desks

I couldn't start teaching immediately, as we had no desks. This problem was overcome when we got some men to cut a few logs and then, by means of cross-cut saws, make some planks out of which we made a table almost as long as the house. The table was used as a substitute for desks. With other planks we made some benches for the children to sit on.

On my first day of teaching I had a few problems. A number of children appeared for class, including two babies in the care of a couple of teenagers. Crying babies and teaching didn't mix well, so I sent the babies home.

All my pupils had Indian nicknames. It is true that some had Christian names, but these were rarely used. Little by little I got them to remember their proper names. At first if I said "Mike, come here," nobody came. But when I said "Big Boy, come here," up came a little fellow. Kitchi Kewizance (Big Boy) was the boy's Indian name. In fact, even today he still goes by that name.

Bon Jour

The following is an extract from my diary: "Our people attend the Sunday Mass very attentively. Nearly all of them prefer to squat on the floor instead of sitting on the school bench. Some of the babies are squalling most of the time, but we are getting used to that."

On one occasion, a fine old man, Charley Dunsford, entered whilst Father de Grandpré was preaching his Sunday sermon. Charley, wishing to show his good manners, went up to Father and shook hands with him, at the same time saying, "bon jour, bon jour." Father said "bon jour" also a couple of times whilst shaking hands and then continued his sermon.

…Father de Grandpré was never idle. Apart from giving instructions to those at Little Grand Rapids, he visited several other reserves. During that winter from December 6 up to the third week in March, he traveled slightly over one-thousand miles with his dogs. Apart from making trips to Bloodvein, Jack Head, Fisher River, and Berens River, he visited Deer Lake and Pikangikum.

It was the first time that members of these previously named Reserves had ever seen a priest. They had been visited a few times by the Reverend Fred Stevens, a minister of the Methodist Church. This gentleman spent most of his time among the Indians and spoke their language fluently. His home mission was Fisher River. He died a number of years ago whilst on his missionary trips.

Travel by Dog Team

It must not be thought that on these long trips during the winter, the missionary just had to sit on the toboggan or sleigh and let his dogs do all the work. It is true that, at times, he might be able to ride short distances, but most of the trip he had to run behind and help guide the toboggan through narrow, twisting bush paths. Food and bedding for the driver, and fish food for the dogs, took up most of the room on the toboggan. Each dog was fed six or seven tulibees at the end of the day's run. [A tulibee is a small variety of whitefish.]

Sometimes during long trips they would get an extra fish at midday. So, you see that on a six-day trip it took nearly 200 fish to feed the dogs.

Horses

During the winter of 1926 to 1927, a Little Grand Rapids trader had been hauling his supplies with a team of horses. For this purpose he had to cut a bush road from Bloodvein to Little Grand Rapids. When the horses arrived for the first time, there was considerable excitement among the children who had never seen one before. "They look like moose" was the remark made by one little fellow.

Trip for Mail

Little Grand Rapids now has a post office, but in those days our nearest one was Berens River. So when we wished to send or receive mail, we had to make a round trip of just about 250 miles. We went by bush road to Bloodvein, a distance of slightly over seventy miles. Then we followed the East Shore of Lake Winnipeg up to Berens, which meant another fifty-five miles.

That winter Father de Grandpré and Mr. Dave Donaldson, the Hudson's Bay clerk, had made their trips for the mail, so my turn came during the third week of March. On the 19th of that same month, I got up at 4:30 a.m., made some bannock, packed up a grub box, rolled up my bedding, filled up a bag of fish for the dogs, then hitched them up and started off. We did fairly well that day and camped outside, a mile from Big Mud Lake. The following morning we were on the move again at 6:30 a.m. From my diary I read, "Hit my knee today. Our road was very bad for about four hours. The muskeg is tiring to travel through. The path is cut along the sunny side. We made two fires on the road and reached Bloodvein at 5:10 p.m."

Monday, March 21. "Started off from Bloodvein at 4:00 a.m. Took a short rest at Rabbit Point, which was reached at 7:00 a.m. Had lunch at Flour Point and Pigeon Point. It was hard going during the day, as there was a thaw and the dogs were tired. Reached Berens River at 7:45 p.m. Distance that day 55 miles. My knee still troubles me considerably."

Life at Little Grand Rapids

In spite of little hardships, life at Little Grand Rapids was pleasant and enjoyable. The Indians were easy to get along with; there was no drinking on the Reserve, which is, unfortunately, not the case today. The children were a nice group of youngsters and made fair progress in school. Another factor that made life agreeable was the friendly co-operation of the staff of the Hudson's Bay Company and Mr. and Mrs. John James Everett, who were in charge of the United Church Mission. In 1968, at the age of seventy-six, Mr. Everett was still working among the Indians at Pikangikum. Even the Indian "medicine men," after a short period, showed no antipathy. In fact, it was at that time I started to take a keen interest in the roots and herbs used by them for various ailments. We thought that we had a tough job when we hauled our freight, by canoe, from Berens to Little Grand Rapids. That was nothing when compared to the trips which had to be made, with supplies, when the Little Grand Rapids Post was opened in 1865. In those days all the supplies for the store were shipped from York Factory. Several hundreds of miles separated these two places.

Improved Mail Service on Lake Winnipeg

Our mail service had also improved. It now started from Berens River. A team of horses was used instead of dogs. The mailman had a sleigh. On the forepart there was a small caboose just big enough to install a small heater and sufficient room for the mailbags. On the rear of the sleigh a limited quantity of freight could be carried. Father de Grandpré also quit using dogs. He had a small sleigh drawn by a single horse. But it does not matter what type of vehicle is used. There is always a certain amount of danger when making trips on Lake Winnipeg.

...During the winter, but more so towards spring, due to contraction and expansion, large cracks form in the ice on Lake Winnipeg. On one occasion our mailman encountered one of these about three miles south of a small settlement. Finding what he thought to be a safe place to cross, he cautiously advanced. The crossing was not as safe as he had thought and his horses fell through the crack. The man was all alone. In spite of every effort made to save the team, they were drowned. In struggling to save them, he got soaked almost halfway up his body. He started to walk towards the little settlement. Soon his clothes started to freeze. Luckily one of the settlers had noticed his plight and drove out with a dog train, probably saving the mailman's life.

Frederick Disbrowe

During the years I spent at Berens River, one of my very good friends was Mr. Frederick Disbrowe. For about twenty-five years he was manager of the Hudson's Bay Company store at Berens. After his retirement, I often used to go and visit him at his home. Chatting with him was always interesting, as he frequently spoke about his younger days [and his time in Middleton's Army during the Metis uprising].

...Mr. Disbrowe was the son of a Canon of the Church of England. When the uprising of the Metis had been settled, he obtained work as a clerk in a fish company doing business on Lake Winnipeg. Later on he became one of the first teachers in the Indian School at Poplar River, after which he obtained his position with the Hudson's Bay Company until he retired. For several years he was also Police Magistrate for this area.

Endnotes to Chapters and Appendices

1. The German translation is as follows:
    Wie koent ich ruhig schlafen in dunkler Nacht;
    Wenn ich O Gott und Vater nicht dein gedacht;
    Es hat des Tages treiben mein Herz zerstreut;
    Bei dir bei dir alleine ist Frieden und Seligkeit. [See Chapter 1].

2. Lothar Schuetze studied at the Lutheran Seminary in Wiesbaden, Germany. His courses were in medicine, pharmacy, and theology. [See Chapter 1].

3. John W. Niddrie (1863-1940), of Presbyterian background, came to Canada from Scotland in 1885. While still in Scotland, Niddrie converted to Methodism. In Canada, he was the principal of the Indian Residential School at Morley, Alberta, for seven years, where he connected closely with John McDougall. He spent the rest of his life among the Anishinabe in the Lake Winnipeg area, seven years at Island Lake, six years at Oxford House, and twenty years at Berens River. Niddrie spoke the Anishinabe language fluently. [See Chapter 2].

4. Luther Schuetze adopted his sister's son when her husband abandoned his family. [See Chapter 2].

5. Square metal box-like heaters with stovepipes going to the chimney, using wood for fuel. After a good fire was made, the draft could be closed and these airtight heaters glowed all night, giving off a certain amount of warmth. [See Chapter 4].

6. Between 1926 and 1929, Schuetze ordered such supplies as beans, rice, peas, pot barley, salt, cocoa, condensed milk, baking soda, a cooking pot, cups, plates, and spoons. He also ordered cleaning supplies, towels, yarn, combs, and soap. The Department of Indian Affairs filled all of these orders. [See Chapter 4].

7. It was August 11, 1929, that the fire crossed the river and was burning toward the mission and schoolhouse at nightfall, according

to the *Little Grand Rapids Post Journal*. On microfilm (See Big Fall, B.18/A10) in the Hudson's Bay Company Archives (HBCA) at the Manitoba Archives. [See Chapter 6].

8. By August 16, 1929, the *Berens River Post Journal* (HBCA) reported, "Store and dwelling house of R.F. Schuetze burned to the ground and all of the Indian Houses on the south side of the river destroyed." [See Chapter 6].

9. A trap comprising a weight balanced on a mechanism made from three pieces of wood interconnected in the shape of a 4 such that the construction collapses when an animal brushes against it. [See Chapter 6].

10. In June, 1929, Schuetze still did not have the desks he had ordered because the Department thought the cost of freight for such heavy supplies was too high. When Schuetze offered to freight them free of charge from Matheson Island, the Department sent 30 desks. [See Chapter 6].

11. The Little Grand Rapids register of baptisms, marriages, and deaths is available at the United Church of Canada: Archives of the Conference of Manitoba and Northwestern Ontario in Winnipeg. Schuetze's entries are included there. [See Chapter 7].

12. The whole story is placed here, though the building was not completed until years later. The planning began in 1930–31, and keeping the story together seemed advisable. [See Chapter 7].

13. The Little Grand Rapids register shows that in 1929 Schuetze baptized the following children: Little Grand Rapids (9); Bloodvein (1); Little Goose Lake (1); Poplar Hill (1); and Pauingassi (14). [See Chapter 7].

14. The Little Grand Rapids register contains the following entry for James Kirkness: Born at Oxford House, died 11 January 1934, buried by Luther Schuetze. [See Chapter 10].

15. The Little Grand Rapids register indicates that Joe Potvin began to witness marriages in 1934. [See Chapter 11].

16. The *Little Grand Rapids Post Journal* mentions that Geiger hauled freight. [See Chapter 11].

17. The second team came out for the building of the church. [See Chapter 11].

18. The *Little Grand Rapids Post Journal* notes that the treaty party left for Pikangikum in June, 1936. [See Chapter 12].

19. According to the HBCA records, John Robert Moar retired on May 31, 1932, and was followed by a Mr. Leslie, who was replaced by J. Stewart in 1936. [See Chapter 13].

20. The *Little Grand Rapids Post Journal* indicates that Thorwaldson was a free-trader. In the summer of 1937 he and his family moved into the house built for Roderick McDonald. [See Chapter 14].

21. See A. Irving Hallowell, *The Ojibwa of Berens River, Manitoba: Ethnography into History* (Fort Worth: Harcourt Brace College Publishers, 1992). [See Chapter 14].

22. The Little Grand Rapids register indicates that John Robert Bear, age 34, married Mary Boucher, age 14, in 1933. [See Chapter 14].

23. Brother Frederick Leach, *60 Years with Indians and Settlers on Lake Winnipeg*. The Oblates of Mary Immaculate, St. Boniface, Manitoba. Pp. 22–35. [See Appendix C].

INDEX